David Cobb, has been a practising Advocate since 1997, and is an experienced and enthusiastic practitioner with expertise in relation to Mental Health, Adults with Incapacity and Human Rights Law. He has written three published textbooks on the evolving area of Mental Health Law in Scotland, and has contributed to the "Scots Law Times" on significant new cases. David's other writing projects include a new updating the Mental Health and Planning sections of the "Scottish Human Rights Service".

David provided advice to the Scottish Government's Independent Review of Learning Disability and Autism in the Mental Health Act (IMRHA) which was published in December 2019. He is a frequent Speaker at Courses and Conferences, and has been a Trustee of a Mental Health Advocacy Charity since 2017.

Since 2024, David has been a Legal Member of the Social Security Chamber in Scotland and a Legally Qualified Chair of Fitness to Practice Hearings for the Scottish Social

# A Practical Guide to the Sheriff Court and Protecting Vulnerable Adults in Scotland

Second Edition

# A Practical Guide to the Sheriff Court and Protecting Vulnerable Adults in Scotland

## Second Edition

David W Cobb
Advocate,
LL.B (Hons) (Edin)

Law Brief Publishing

Published 2024 by Law Brief Publishing, an imprint of Law Brief Publishing Ltd
30 The Parks
Minehead
Somerset
TA24 8BT

www.lawbriefpublishing.com

Paperback: 978-1-916698-63-5

*To Linda, Adam and Neil for their support throughout my career and also to the late Pat and Harry Cobb who saw their Son become a Lawyer.*

*The assistance of Sandra McDonald, former Public Guardian for Scotland and Adrian Ward in allowing quotation from their publications is gratefully acknowledged.*

# PREFACE

It is not always simple to recognise how changes in society and changes in law can be reflected in a dynamic and continuing process. The subject of this short textbook is one which languished for a long time, archaic and disregarded, in a relatively obscure and specialist corner. One purpose of this work will be to demonstrate the increasing centrality of the law concerning adults with incapacity to many of us, whether as individual, family member, friend or professional. It will also consider the emerging future direction of legislation.

The law in Scotland applying to adults with incapacity (AWI) has progressed immeasurably from a limited and generally inaccessible jurisdiction to one which aspires to reflect the absorption of human rights into national jurisprudence. However, in the time which has elapsed since the principal legislation, the Adults with Incapacity (Scotland) Act 2000 ("the 2000 Act") became law, considerable additional considerations have emerged which should drive a further evolution to reflect better contemporary standards and norms.

At the time of writing, the Scottish Government has published proposals for new statutory provisions, stemming from a number of reports, but primarily the Review of Mental Health Law in Scotland, chaired by the distinguished and experienced QC John Scott. The evolution of the thinking behind that document leading to these current proposals is considered in more detail at the end of this work.

However, what has also become apparent recently is that the Scottish Government will not immediately proceed with a previously mooted Human Rights Act, part of which was designed to incorporate the United Nations Convention on the Rights of Persons with Disabilities (CRPD) into domestic Scottish Law, as recently occurred with the United Nations Convention of the Rights of the Child.

For the present therefore, the influence of Human Rights law on future legislation will be one of informing its terms, with the aim of making this compatible with the European Convention on Human Rights. Nevertheless, to take one important example, in the case of authorising deprivation of liberty of an incapable adult, the issue remains outstanding nearly 25 years.

Irrespective of whether the desire to make the CRPD directly enforceable in this jurisdiction has diminished, the number of adults with some form of incapacity, is significant. Remarkably, there is no centrally-held record of what that number is, although a reasonable estimate is that there are currently more that 200,000 adults in Scotland with what is termed a mental incapacity – including dementia and learning disability – which number is forecast to rise inexorably in the future.

However, it is an oversimplification to regard this group as defined simply by a condition such as dementia, significant as that is. People who have a learning disability, alcohol-related brain damage, acquired brain injury or the consequences of a medical event such as a stroke, may equally engage the AWI provisions.

There is, of course, a balance to be struck in response. Many of these conditions should not mandate the imposition of an all-embracing legal regime on an adult on any view, although in more serious cases, there may be little practicable alternative. One question may be whether informal arrangements – characteristically those made by family members or friends – or the provision of adequate independent advocacy support will suffice in some circumstances.

A critical issue in striking the proper balance is the extent to which the adult remains able to control decision – making in their day-to-day life, as opposed to having this done on their behalf. The current law primarily offers pathways, whether by an adult themselves or via the courts, to bring about the latter outcome, but the direction of travel envisages an increasing role for supported decision-making by an adult as opposed to their agency being exercised via a substitute.

There is also a forward-looking element in such matters, insofar as many will wish to ensure what arrangements would operate in the event of a loss of capacity for some reason, irrespective of whether the situation actually arises. Ultimately, these are some of the things more conventionally determined by a will on death, but such instruments rarely establish what should happen during the granter's lifetime.

It is important therefore, that families, practitioners and related professionals understand what the law is, how it currently operates, and also how it may develop in the future. The aim of this text is to explain and hopefully make straightforward the ways in which the law can assist in striking a proper balance of the exercise of agency for each individual concerned.

The law quoted is accurate up to 31 July 2024. For the sake of clarification, references made to the Practice Note of Lothian and Borders are intended to illustrate by way of example the approach taken in that jurisdiction to Applications made under the 2000 Act. Practitioners should familiarise themselves with any equivalent document applying within their particular Sheriffdom.

*David Cobb*
*November 2024*

# CONTENTS

# CHAPTER ONE

# TOWARDS THE 2000 ACT

Historically, interventions in the affairs of those described as "fools and idiots", "furious" or "prodigal" required to be authorised via the Court of Session – the Supreme Court in Scotland – exercising powers under common law, as what was termed its *parens patriae.* Thus, individuals could apply to the Court for appointment to the office of tutor-at-law, or later, *curator bonis* to an adult [1].

The expense and effort of obtaining such appointments meant that these occurred relatively rarely, and scope for misuse or outright exploitation resulting from the unequal bargaining power of the parties undoubtedly existed. Equally daunting was undertaking any initiative to restore capacity to the individual concerned.

Whilst such appointees were subject to the supervision of the Court, the function of a *curator bonis* was essentially confined to preserving the estate of the individual or ward. This essentially negative power meant that steps to invest or acquire property were unlikely to occur.

A form of statutory guardianship was brought into force by the Mental Health (Scotland) Act 1984 [2]. Section 92 of the 1984 Act allowed a local authority to petition to be appointed as *curator bonis* to an adult "incapable by reason of mental disorder", which proved operable only in a limited fashion. The absence of any fuller regime for the management of an adult's affairs resulted briefly in an innovative and successful application for appointment of a tutor dative to an adult [3].

Even then, many of the considerations previously applying to other appointments made under common law applied equally to a tutor dative. Thus, the law maintained a system which was inaccessible and difficult to review; imposed an all or nothing divestiture of legal agency, and required only a limited relationship to exist between a *curator bonis* and the adult [4].

Remarkably, this regime remained in place until the dawn of the 21st century. It may be that pressures on passing substantial Scottish legislation through the Westminster Parliament was instrumental in delaying reform in this field. However, the establishment of the Holyrood Parliament in 1999 undoubtedly created more scope for more rapid and substantial change.

As is considered later, what originally existed was far from compatible with European Convention on Human Rights (EConHR) as incorporated by the Human Rights Act 1998 [5]. It is arguable that articles 5 (Deprivation of liberty), 6 (Access to a court) 8 (respect for family and private life) and Protocol 1, Article 1 of the Convention would have been infringed by the common law [6].

By this point, steps toward reform already had been taken in the shape of the Scottish law commission report on *Incapable adults* [7]. In turn, this resulted in the 2000 Act, arguably the first major legislation passed by the Holyrood Parliament which addressed the new human rights requirements, and which took effect on 1st April 2002.

The 2000 Act itself was the subject of some amendment and modification by the Adult Support and Protection (Scotland) Act 2007 ("the 2007 Act") [8], but the former remains the principal statute for the purposes of this work.

As an introduction to the changes it effected, the following were established in the wake of enactment of the 2000 Act:-

- A definition was provided of "incapacity" [9].

- Statutory provision was made regulating the making and operation of a power of attorney on both a continuing and welfare basis [10].

- The office of guardian was considerably widened, and a formal distinction made between a financial guardian and a welfare guardian [11].
- A specific and limited form of guardianship was introduced in the form of an intervention order [12].
- The Sheriff Court was established as the court of primary jurisdiction in relation to guardianship, and new procedures for making appropriate applications established [13].
- The Office of the public guardian ("OPG") was created alongside arrangements for the management of estates and registration supervision of powers of attorney, as also supervision of the conduct of guardianship and intervention orders [14].

While the whole range of the Law in Scotland concerning Mental Health and Capacity Law in Scotland has received consideration by the Review of Mental Health Law in Scotland [15], and consultation on possible reforms are in progress at the time of writing, and are considered at the end of this work. However, for the moment, the 2000 Act remains the core statute concerning the legal rights of and support for adults with incapacity in Scotland.

## NOTES (CHAPTER 1)

1. For a more detailed study of the history of the common law regime, see Adrian Ward, *Adult Incapacity* (SULI) (2003).

2. S.92 of the 1984 Act allowed a local authority to petition to be appointed as *curator bonis* to an adult "incapable by reason of mental disorder".

3. *Morris Petitioner* (1986) (Unreported).

4. A very limited power of *negotiorum gestio* continues to be recognised at common law, which can be regarded as limited only to situations of urgency or emergency.

5. Section 6 of the 1998 Act makes it unlawful for a "public authority" to act in a way which is incompatible with a Convention right.

6. For further consideration of the effects of the 1998 Act, see Chapter 19 below.

7. SLC *Report on Incapable Adults* (No.151) (1995).

8. See, for example, the substantially revised provisions regarding to Authority to Intromit considered in Chapter 16 below.

9. See Chapter 2 below.

10. See Chapters 5, 6, 7 & 17 below.

11. See Chapter 9 below.

12. See Chapter 14 below.

13. See Chapter 9 below.

14. See Chapters 7 & 17 below.

15. *Scottish Mental Health Law Review* (September 2022), which is more generally referred to as "the Scott Review" (See Chapter 24 below). As is also considered later, incorporation of the UN Convention on the Rights of Persons with Disability (UNCRPD) into the domestic law of Scotland via a Human Rights Act is under a measure of active consideration.

# CHAPTER TWO

# INCAPACITY AND THE 2000 ACT

For the purposes of the 2000 Act, an "adult" is a person who has attained the age of 16 years [1]. The definition of an "adult's" "incapacity" provided in the 2000 Act is to the effect that it:

> "means incapable of–
>
> (a) acting; or
>
> (b) making decisions; or
>
> (c) communicating decisions; or
>
> (d) understanding decisions; or
>
> (e) retaining the memory of decisions,
>
> as mentioned in any provision of this Act, by reason of mental disorder or of inability to communicate because of physical disability; but a person shall not fall within this definition by reason only of a lack or deficiency in a faculty of communication if that lack or deficiency can be made good by human or mechanical aid (whether of an interpretative nature or otherwise)" [2].

It will be noted that an adult can meet this definition not merely by having a "mental disorder" but also as the result of a physical disability (for example, an acquired brain injury), which renders communication of wishes and feelings impracticable or impossible.

A "mental disorder" is set out in s.328 of the Mental Health (Care and Treatment) (Scotland) Act 2003 ("the 2003 Act") which specifies the following:-

> "(a) mental illness;
>
> (b) personality disorder; or
>
> (c) learning disability,
>
> however caused or manifested;" [3].

Section 328 also defines conditions which do *not* amount to a "mental disorder", namely:-

> "(a) sexual orientation;
>
> (b) sexual deviancy;
>
> (c) transsexualism;
>
> (d) transvestism;
>
> (e) dependence on, or use of, alcohol or drugs;
>
> (f) behaviour that causes, or is likely to cause, harassment, alarm or distress to any other person;
>
> (g) acting as no prudent person would act." [4].

Consequently, the *Code of practice for local authorities* issued by the Scottish government under the 2000 Act provides a number of instances where an individual who, for example, receives community care services; has difficulties with speech or writing, or has a poor memory, will not normally meet the criteria to establish "incapacity" [5]. It follows that measures which cannot be authorised under the 2003 Act for reason of absence of a "mental disorder", equally cannot be authorised under the

2000 Act, unless one or more of the criteria for physical disability are satisfied [6].

It is instructive to compare the definition of "incapacity" given in the 2000 Act with the benchmark provided in England and Wales by the Mental Capacity Act 2005, which states that:-

> "A person is not to be treated as unable to make a decision unless *all practicable steps to help him have been taken without success"* (Emphasis added) [7].

What is made clear by that definition, and it is submitted is also the case in Scotland, is that determining "incapacity" in relation to a given situation or decision does not mandate an all or nothing approach. One simple example is that an adult may not be capable of deciding where to go on holiday, but perfectly capable of deciding what clothes to wear day by day [8]. For that purpose, the bar to be cleared to establish "incapacity" may rest at a somewhat higher level than merely encouraging an adult to use their skills concerning their affairs to the greatest degree possible [9].

As mentioned in the preface, to regard the 2000 Act as being solely concerned with adults who have dementia or a learning disability is to adopt an over narrow approach. In practice, such conditions will be the background to many orders made and actions taken under this legislation, but sight must not be lost of its potential or its applicability to other groups.

However, exercise of any of the powers created by the 2000 Act essentially are contingent upon – in the various manners considered later – an adult meeting the specified test of "incapacity". To take two examples, the appointment of someone to act under a power of attorney may only be triggered at a point when the granter has become "incapable" [10]. Similarly, the Sheriff may only grant a guardianship or intervention order where satisfied that the adult concerned is:

> "incapable in relation to decision about, or of acting to safeguard or promote his interests in, his property, financial affairs or personal welfare, and is likely to continue to be incapable." [11].

In the present system in Scotland, such assessment primarily will stem from the opinion of a medically qualified practitioner [12]. Ultimately, the Sheriff Court is empowered to determine any dispute as to the "incapacity" of an adult [13].

An example of how the test might be assessed was given by Sheriff Reith in *City of Edinburgh Council v D* [14].

> "In the light of the evidence, including the evidence of the respondent himself, I am satisfied that the respondent can "make" at least some decisions. For example, he has instructed solicitors to represent him in relation to the present applications. He has also "decided" that he does not wish to move to Blackfriars Street. That said, in the light of Dr Carson's evidence, it may be debatable whether the respondent is really capable of "making" decisions in relation to his interests in his personal welfare in the sense of being able to "form a balanced judgement", as referred to by Dr Carson. However, in the view of the fact that the respondent can technically "make" decisions, it may be that the respondent's condition falls more properly under the heading of "understanding" decisions in section 1(6)(d). In my opinion, it is certainly that in any event. I shall therefore proceed on that basis. I would also add that I accepted [the] submission that section 1(6) is not about the quality of decisions, and that the issue is one of "incapacity" and not one of "poor choices". I have therefore also approached matters on this basis." [15].

Nevertheless, it is important to recognise that the common law will not necessarily apply the test of the 2000 Act to matters such as capacity to make a will [16].

## NOTES (CHAPTER 2)

1. 2000 Act, s1(6). It is possible to apply for a Guardianship order three months in advance of a child attaining the age of 16 (2000 Act, s.79A). See Chapter 8 below. The UNCRC (Incorporation) (Scotland) Act 2024 specifies that a person is "a child" until reaching the age of 18 (2024 Act, s.1(2), incorporating Convention art.1). The 2024 Act requires a "public authority" not to act, or fail to act, in connection with a "relevant function" in a way which is incompatible with the UNCRC requirement (2024 Act, s.6 (1). A "relevant function" includes a function that is conferred by an Act of the Scottish Parliament (2024 Act, s.6(2)(b)(i)), which necessarily includes the 2000 Act. It cannot be stated certainly at the time of writing how the position of children aged 16 or 17 will be affected by being treated as an "adult" under the 2000 Act. (See also Chapter 4 below).

2. 2000 Act, s.1(6). See FN 7 below.

3. 2000 Act, s.328. The more recent Mental Capacity (NI) Act 2016 does not determine whether an individual has "capacity" only as stemming from a "mental disorder". (2016 Act, s.1). Whether a "learning disability" or autism should be included as forms of "mental disorder" is disputed in some quarters, and may be addressed by the proposed Learning Disabilities, Neurodivergence and Autism Bill which is subject to Consultation at the time of writing (See Chapter [24] below).

4. 2000 Act, s.328.

5. *Code of practice for local authorities*, Scottish Government (2008), Chapter 1. Scottish ministers have the power to issue guidance on interpretation of the 2000 Act in the form of Codes of practice to eight specified groups. Where reference is made to a *Code of practice* in succeeding Chapters, generally it will mean the document relevant to the subject (See also FN 16 in Chapter 3).

6. See FN 11 below.

7. Mental Capacity Act 2005, s.1(3). Whether the current statutory definition of "incapacity" in Scotland generally is fit for modern purpose is a long- term issue being considered by the Scottish Government (See Chapter 24 below).

8. Another example given in the *Code of practice for local authorities* is of an adult capable of deciding which electricity supplier to use but unable to manage the mechanics of changing the supplier.

9. 2000 Act, s.1(5). See the analysis applied by Sheriff Lugton in *D v Falkirk Council 2023 GWD 10-110* regarding whether an Adult with Aspergers had a "mental disorder" which made him "incapable" and see Chapter 3 below.

10. See Chapter 6 below.

11. 2000 Act, ss. 53 (1) & 58 (1) (a). See Chapters 9 & 14 below.

12. See Chapter 23 below. In relation to the provision of certain forms of medical treatment, other professionals are entitled to assess whether an adult is "incapable" for that purpose.

13. 2000 Act, s.14. Decisions of the Sheriff, or on appeal the Sheriff Appeal Court (See Chapter 15 below) can be determined by the Court of Session.

14. 2011 SLT (Sh Ct) 15.

15. At para.162.

16. See *Smyth v Romaine's Execx.* [2014] CSOH 150.

# CHAPTER THREE

# THE FIVE PRINCIPLES

A distinctly innovative part of the 2000 Act was the adoption of a set of broad principles in order to apply them to:-

> "any intervention in the affairs of an adult under or in pursuance of this Act, including any order made in or for the purpose of any proceedings under this Act for or connection with an adult" [1].

It is important to recognise that these principles are to be "given effect" to "*any* intervention" made under the 2000 Act (Emphasis added). While certain office holders are subject to express requirements [2], it is submitted that this wide provision applies to almost anyone bearing to act under colour of the 2000 Act. As such, it arguably embraces almost all of the persons set out in Chapter 4 below.

A: No intervention without benefit to the adult (s.1 (2)):

> "There shall be no intervention in the affairs of an adult unless the person responsible for authorising or effecting the intervention will benefit the adult and that such benefit *cannot reasonably be achieved without the intervention*" [3].

The term "intervention" is not defined further in the 2000 Act. While it clearly connotes a positive action or decision to act, it is further submitted that inaction or a decision *not* to act equally is comprehended by this principle [4]. That conclusion is strengthened by reference to the following two principles.

B: Least restrictive intervention upon the freedom of the adult (s.1 (3)):

> "Where it is determined that an intervention as mentioned [in the first principle] is to be made, such intervention shall be the *least*

> *restrictive option in relation to the freedom of the adult*, consistent with the purpose of the intervention" [5].

The wording of this part of the 2000 Act points towards circumstances where a determination not to act to restrict the ability of an adult to take decisions, or continue in their current living arrangements, is a preferable outcome. For example, were an adult's period of "incapacity" likely to be of a limited duration, major changes – say the sale of shares or jewellery – may prove unnecessarily stressful when capacity is regained.

The expression "benefit" is also undefined in the 2000 Act, and clearly is capable of a wide definition. There may be circumstances where making an intervention would simply worsen the adult's situation, and that "benefit" can be seen to flow simply from doing nothing. It seems to be the case however, that "benefit" need not be one which accrues only to the adult [6].

Similarly, the expression "least restrictive" is capable of a fairly broad interpretation. While there may be an obvious, if rough, hierarchy between allowing an adult to remain in their own home and having them live in a care home within a locked wing, what lies between may be viewed more or less favourably from different perspectives. Some measures will result from wholly voluntary acts of an adult (e.g. the granting of a power of attorney [7]) and others will be imposed by a Court, such as a guardianship order [8].

C: Past wishes and feelings of the adult (s.1 (4) (a)):

The scheme of the 2000 Act presumes against an "intervention" being carried out in a vacuum, particularly with regard to the interests of the adult. Thus, operation of the principles previously set out are amplified in relation to the evaluation of any act or decision as follows:-

> "In determining if an intervention is to be made and, if so, what intervention is to be made, account shall be taken of–

(a) the present and past wishes and feelings of the adult so far as they can be ascertained by any means of communication, whether human or by mechanical aid (whether of an interpretative nature or otherwise) appropriate to the adult;" [9]

D: Views of other interested persons (s.1 (4)(b)-(d))

In making any "intervention" made under the 2000 Act, account also requires to be taken of:-

"(b) the views of the nearest relative, named person and the primary carer of the adult, in so far as it is reasonable and practicable to do so;

(c) the views of—

(i) any guardian, continuing attorney or welfare attorney of the adult who has powers relating to the proposed intervention; and.

(ii) any person whom the sheriff has directed to be consulted,

in so far as it is reasonable and practicable to do so; and

(d) the views of any other person appearing to the person responsible for authorising or effecting the intervention to have an interest in the welfare of the adult or in the proposed intervention, where these views have been made known to the person responsible, in so far as it is reasonable and practicable to do so." [10].

It will be seen therefore, that the first consideration is founded on the wishes and feelings of the adult. That is capable of being expressed in a number of means, ranging from written documents such as a power of attorney or statement of wishes and feelings, to expressions made to professionals to the kind of verbal statements made in day-to-day conversation [11].

What an adult's wishes and preferences have been can be gleaned from a written document, but it is foreseeable that these will not be comprehensive, or may not address subsequent developments, or even that the adult simply has changed their mind on a matter. In such circumstances, the matter of what takes precedence may require careful analysis.

The *Code of practice for persons authorised under intervention orders and guardians* instances examples where an adult may have expressed views which seem contrary to their own interests, such as a person with a severe mental disorder who is determined to spend all their money, or one with a learning disability who is over eager to please a friend or relative and thus is unable to appreciate the value of their possessions [12].

Accordingly, further sources of information are specified to be taken into account "in so far as it is reasonable and practicable" to do so, including those directed by the Sheriff Court. This net is cast even wider where views have been communicated to the person making (or not making) an intervention in the affairs of an adult. [13].

E: Participation by the adult (s.1 (5)):

One specific counterbalance in the favour of an adult's agency is provided to the effect that:-

> "Any guardian, continuing attorney, welfare attorney or manager of an establishment exercising functions under this Act or under any order of the sheriff in relation to an adult shall, in so far as it is reasonable and practicable to do so, encourage the adult to exercise whatever skills he has concerning his property, financial affairs or personal welfare, as the case may be, and to develop new such skills." [14].

Examples of this latter consideration provided by the *Code of Practice for persons authorised under intervention orders or guardians* include, using shops which permit changing booths to be used by spouses or partners;

obtaining a restaurant's menu in advance to provide the choice being made; or use of a befriending system [15].

It will be apparent that a significant difference may arise between how one individual or Court assesses the application of the principles between one given situation from another. As will be considered later, protection from liability can be provided by showing that the five principles have been considered and applied to an "intervention". Such a position is likely to be strengthened if full and adequate records are maintained [16].

As already noted, issues may be clarified by taking into account the detailed advice provided in the *Codes of practice* issued by the Scottish government in conjunction with the 2000 Act, to which reference is made throughout this work. These provide guidance to the subject of each *Code of practice* in the exercise of their respective functions [17].

Such documents cannot be expected to be comprehensive or to anticipate every circumstance. This may make effective challenge to a decision or conclusion problematic, in terms of whether due consideration of the terms of the relevant *Code of practice* took place, or else whether an intervention was sufficiently a departure from such guidance or sufficiently misconceived, so as to violate the five principles.

This may be particularly important in relation to the decision whether to intervene or not and the extent of any intervention which takes place. What seems essential is avoidance of an outright failure to consider whatsoever any relevant passages of statute or advice.

Consequently, the subsequent content of this book requires to be viewed with the existence of the five principles firmly in mind. In simple terms, the existence of a power described does not mean that it must be used, but if it is, it is intended that it will be exercised in conformity with these principles.

A recent example of a Sheriff conducting an exercise of determining which Guardianship powers required to be granted in relation to an adult can be found in *SBC v AB* [18].

Overall, the kind of analysis made there suggests that the application of the five principles mandates particular questions to be asked – and answers provided – prior to embarking (or not) on seeking guardianship over an adult such as:-

- Is it likely that the adult is "incapable"?
- Is there any other means open to achieve the end sought?
- Can the adult's interests be promoted by anything less than a guardianship order being made?
- Could the desired benefit to the adult be obtained without making a guardianship order?
- Is a guardianship order the least restrictive option?
- What views and wishes of the adult are known?

Later parts of this work will consider other relevant considerations, which generally will require to be taken into account in exercising powers in a manner consistent with the five principles. Further, as also considered below, there are instances where the holding of various offices under the 2000 Act requires some level of record – keeping [19].

One final significant issue is that an inevitable consequence of immediate family or close relatives acting under the 2000 Act is that conflicts of interest are likely to arise at times. One obvious example may be where a family member is appointed under a power of attorney, but also has an interest – whether or not as executor – in the estate of the granter of the power of attorney.

Here, to give one example, acts which the attorney considers will benefit the adult – such as their placement in a care home – may impact on what the attorney might receive on the adult's death. Does an attorney who sells a property unaware of bequests made in the adult's will, in effect, change that will? If so, can a solicitor holding the will claim client confidentiality if the attorney wishes to check the position?

In practice, situations may occur where mismanagement of an adult's estate under a power of attorney, significantly impacts on the entitlement of beneficiaries under the adult's will. While often a sensitive matter, appointment of different individuals to the position of attorney and executor may seem a practicable means of avoiding such outcomes.

These kinds of practical issues may need resolution in the course of conducting the functions this work will consider. In this regard, sight should not be lost of the right of *any* person "claiming an interest in the property, financial affairs or welfare of an adult intervene" in the exercise of functions or the making of orders under the 2000 Act [20].

## NOTES (CHAPTER 3)

1. 2000 Act, s1 (1).

2. See Chapter 4 below and 2000 Act, s.1 (5) & (7).

3. 2000 Act, s.1 (2). Emphasis added.

4. in *D v Falkirk Council 2023 GWD 10-110*, the Sheriff held that the terms of the 2000 Act were sufficiently broad to comprehend an "intervention" being authorised on an anticipatory basis (at paras. 14 &15)

5. 2000 Act, s.1 (3).

6. See *B's Curator Bonis, Noter* 1996 SLT (Sh.Ct.) 27, where the Court allowed a *curator bonis* to sign a variation passing part of the adult's estate falling to the ward's husband to their sons, thereby reducing a prospective inheritance tax liability. (See also *T Applicant* 2005 SLT (Sh.Ct.) 97, and the analysis by the Sheriff of the approach of the public guardian to the issue of "benefit").

7. See Chapter 5 below.

8. In relation to the making of a guardianship order (See Chapter 9 below), the Court must be satisfied that:- "no other means under this Act would be sufficient to enable the adult's interests…to be safeguarded or promoted" (2000 Act, s.58 (1) (b)).

9. In *D v Falkirk Council*, the Sheriff noted that the requirement of s.1 (4) of the 2000 Act to take account of the Adult's views was expressed in unqualified terms which suggested that the duty was of an unqualified nature (At para.16).

10. 2000 Act, s.1 (4). The broad wording of this provision has given rise to significant divergence in the practice of Sheriffs regarding whose views should be sought; in some cases resulting in delays in

proceeding. At the time of writing, the Scottish Government is considering whether more specific guidance should be included in future provisions. (See FN 21 below).

11. See Chapter 7 below. Other possible sources of an adult's wishes and feelings include an advance statement (See 2003 Act, s.275) and will, if accessible.

12. *Code of Practice for persons authorised to act under intervention orders and guardians*, Scottish government (2008) para.4.43.

13. 2000 Act, s.1 (4)(c).

14. 2000 Act, s.1 (4)(d).

15. 2000 Act, s.1 (5).

16. *Code of Practice for persons authorised under intervention orders or guardians*, Scottish government (2008), para.6.51.

17. See Chapters 7 & 10 below.

18. 2000 Act, s.13. This section empowers Scottish Ministers to issue *Codes of practice* regarding the exercise of functions by local authorities and their chief social work officers and mental health officers; continuing and welfare attorneys; persons authorised under intervention orders; guardians; withdrawers; managers of authorised establishments; supervisory bodies; persons authorised to carry out medical treatment or research under Part 5 of the 2000 Act. Each of these offices will be considered later in this text. It should be noted that several *Codes of practice* date from before 2010 and the most recent is the *Code of practice for financial and welfare attorneys* which was updated in 2018.

19. 2020 SLT (Sh.Ct.) 41. See also *City of Edinburgh Council v D* 2011 SLT (Sh.Ct.) 15, where Sheriff Reith provides an example

of how the various principles can be evaluated and balanced (At paras.181-183).

20. These will include the fiduciary duty; the duty of care; the duty of confidentiality (See Chapter 7 below), advice issued by the public guardian (2000 Act, s.6(2) (e)), and also whether the provision offering relief from liability (2000 Act, s.82) can be utilised (See Chapter 17 below).

21. See in particular 2000 Act, ss.3, 20, 25, 53 & 57. One example can be found in *B's Guardian, Minuter 2010 GWD 33- 690.* In *B Minuter* 2015 SLT (Sh.Ct.) 5, Sheriff Baird observed that the category of persons who might have an interest in an adult under this provision had been deliberately left very wide (At para.10). It may also be useful to keep in mind whether advice can be sourced from the public guardian in such circumstances.

# CHAPTER FOUR

# WHO IS INVOLVED?

There are a number of key roles under the 2000 Act which require further definition.

Statutory capacities

**Adult**

A person over age 16 who is "incapable" [1].

**Attorney**

The person(s) appointed to act under a power of attorney (An attorney may exercise continuing / or welfare powers according to the terms of the relative power of attorney [2].

**Guardian**

The person(s) appointed under a guardianship order made by the Sheriff Court (A guardian may exercise financial and / or welfare powers according to the terms of their appointment. Joint guardians or substitute guardians can also discharge the role [3].

**Intervener**

A person authorised to take any action authorised by an intervention order (An intervener can exercise financial and / or welfare powers according to the terms of their appointment [4].

**Withdrawer**

A person authorised to deal with funds belonging to an adult [5].

**Appointee**

A person authorised to receive DWP benefits on behalf of an adult [6].

Individual Capacities

**Nearest relative**

The identity of a "nearest relative" is established by reference to a list set out in the 2003 Act, s.254. The person acting as "nearest relative" can be removed from this capacity by the Court of Session or Sheriff [7].

**Named person**

The means by which a natural person becomes the named person of an adult is set out in the 2003 Act ss.250. & 258. Appointment stems from nomination by an adult and written acceptance by the nominee. An application for removal of an individual from the position of named person can be made to the Mental Health Tribunal for Scotland (MHTS) by various people, including the adult or their guardian or welfare attorney [8].

**Primary carer**

The person or organisation "primarily engaged" in providing care for the adult [9].

Official Capacities

**Office of the public guardian (OPG)**

The statutory supervisor of the conduct of the estates of adults with incapacity, including responsibility for the registration of orders made under the 2000 Act. (The office holder is referred to as "the public guardian") [10]. The public guardian maintains a website public-guardian.gov.uk and an X (Twitter) account.

## Local authorities

Any local authority established under the Local Government Etc (Scotland) 1994. In practice, many relevant social work functions may be carried out via a joint local authority / NHS health and social care partnership (HSCP) [11].

## Mental welfare commission for Scotland (MWCS)

Initially established under the Mental Health (Scotland) Act 1984, the powers and responsibilities of the MWCS are specified in ss.4-20 of the 2003 Act, as amended, and include functions conferred on MWCS by the 2000 Act [12]. The MWCS maintains a website mwcscot.org.uk and an X (Twitter) account.

## Chief social work officer (CWSO)

Each local authority is required to appoint a CSWO for the purposes of carrying out their functions under the Social Work (Scotland) Act 1968 [13]. In certain instances arising under the 2000 Act, the CSWO is required to act as a default party in order to protect the welfare of an incapable adult.

## Mental health officer (MHO)

An MHO is an appointee of a local authority, but exercises functions under both the 2000 and 2003 Act, where the MHO operates independently [14].

## Independent advocacy service

Independently run organisations charged with providing

> "services of support and representation made available for the purpose of enabling the person to whom they are available to have as much control, or capacity to influence, that person's care and welfare as is, in the circumstances, appropriate" [15]

## Safeguarder

This normally is a solicitor, advocate or social worker appointed by the Sheriff Court "for the purpose of safeguarding the interests of the person who is the subject of [an] application or proceedings". This includes "conveying [the person's] views, so far as they are ascertainable to the Sheriff", albeit this particular duty can also be assigned elsewhere where the Sheriff considers it "inappropriate" for the appointed safeguarder to do so [16].

In *Boyle v Denton* [17], the Sheriff Appeal Court clarified that the role of a safeguarder was not merely to express the adult's wishes and feelings, nor was it to carry out the functions of an expert witness (See *Kennedy v Cordia Services LLP 2016 SC (UKSC) 59*): it was to safeguard the interests of the adult and to report to the court; in practice, a safeguarder would usually review the application, interview relevant parties, meet the applicant(s) and the adult, prepare a report, and comment on the application in so far as its effect on the interests of the adult; the safeguarder could also appear at any Hearing [18].

## Medical practitioner

For the purposes of the 2000 Act, certain certificates require to be issued by a "relevant medical practitioner". A "medical practitioner" must first be registered with the general medical council [19], but then requires to be listed by a health board as having met prescribed qualifications and experience and undertaken training. Such a list must be maintained by a health board in Scotland [20]. Certain other professionals are entitled to authorise the giving of forms of medical treatment to an adult under the 2000 Act [21].

## Sheriff

With certain limited exceptions, the Sheriff Court exclusively deals with matters arising under the 2000 Act, including applications for granting of guardianship orders and intervention orders or for directions [22]. The

Sheriff also deals with referrals of disputes from matters subject to the public guardian's jurisdiction [23].

Appeals from decisions of the Sheriff can be made to the Sheriff Appeal Court and thereafter, the Court of Session [24].

It is submitted that all of the persons described above require expressly to follow the five principles in their actings and decisions in relation to an adult with incapacity, although those listed are not exhaustive of those subject to such obligations. Recently, the rationale of the structure of the 2000 Act and the responsibilities assigned were described thus:-

> "..[The] structure of the Act, the safeguards built into it, in the form of the supervisory functions given to the public guardian and the local authority, overseen in the case of the latter by [MWCS]..a guardianship order may only be made by a judicial officer, and only when satisfied in respect of stringent statutory requirement, which require to be interpreted according to the principles of minimal intervention, in the best interests of the adult, taking account as far as possible his or her wishes, all as specified in s.1 of the Act" [25].

This judicial overview is a useful summary to bear in mind when considering the overall operation of the 2000 Act.

## NOTES (CHAPTER 4)

1. See Chapter 2, FN1 above.

2. See 2000 Act, s.15 and Chapter 5 below.

3. See 2000 Act, ss.57, 62 & 63 and Chapter 12 below.

4. See 2000 Act, s.53 (5) and Chapter 14 below.

5. 2000 Act, ss.24A – 33, as amended. See Chapter 16 below.

6. See Chapter 16 below.

7. 2000 Act s.4. See also LM v Renfrewshire Council 2024 SLT (SAC) 55. The Sheriff Appeal Court observed that the language of s.87 of the 2000 Act, applying s.254 of the Mental Health (Care and Treatment) (Scotland) Act 2003, pointed to appointment of a "nearest relative" being made in the singular (At para.29).

8. 2003 Act, s.256. The right to apply to MHTS attaches equally to a financial guardian and welfare guardian.

9. 2000 Act, s.87. See, however, *Ward Appellant* 2014 SLT (Sh.Ct.) 15 at para.4.

10. 2000 Act, ss.6 & 7.

11. HSCPs are bodies established under the Public Bodies (Joint Working) (Scotland) Act 2014. See also 2000 Act, s.9 (4) & (5).

12. 2000 Act, s.9. See also 2003 Act, s.4 (2).

13. Social Work (Scotland) Act 1968, s.3.

14. 2003 Act, s.32. See *Aberdeenshire Council v JM* 2017 SLT 1181 at 1188H.

15. See 2003 Act, s.259 (5). In making decisions under the 2000 Act, the Sheriff must take account of any views of the adult as expressed via an independent advocacy service (2000 Act, s.3 (5A)).

16. 2000 Act, s.3 (4). The Sheriff Court retains the power at common law to appoint a *curator ad litem*. However, the decision of the Court of Protection of England and Wales in *Aberdeenshire Council v SF (No.2) [2024] EWCOP 10* (See Chapter 20 below) may result in appointment of a Safeguarder being required where an Adult is unable themself to express their views on a guardianship application. At the time of writing, the Scottish Government is considering whether to specify the duties of Safeguarders and Curators ad litem in Regulations.

17. *2024 SLT (SAC) 113.*

18. At para.40.

19. 2003 Act, s.329 (1).

20. 2003 Act, s.22 (1) and 2000 Act s.57(6B) (a). See *H Applicant* 2007 SLT (Sh.Ct.) 5, which confirmed that the medical practitioner requires to be registered with a health board in Scotland in order to exercise functions in Scotland under the 2000 Act. (See 2000 Act s.57(6B) (b) regarding the required qualifications and consultation with MWCS in relation to circumstances where an adult is outwith Scotland).

21. See Chapter 23 below.

22. See Chapters 9 and 14 below. The Sheriff also has broad powers to issue Directions under s.3 of the 2000 Act.

23. See Chapter 17 below.

24. See Chapter 15 below. In *JK v Argyll and Bute Council 2022 SC 235*, the Sheriff Appeal Court confirmed that the statutory route

for making Appeals under the 2000 Act was as provided by s.2 (3) (At para.11).

25. *Aberdeenshire Council v JM*, per LJC Dorrian at 1189.

# CHAPTER FIVE

# OBTAINING POWER OF ATTORNEY

For a considerable amount of time, it has been possible for an adult to grant a document authorising another adult to manage all or some of their affairs or finances. The document which gives this effect is called a power of attorney. During 2022-23, the public guardian had registered 77,441 powers of attorney, reflecting a significantly upward trend from previous years, possibly due to better publicity of the service and the clearing of a backlog caused by the COVID pandemic. 76,760 of those registered contained both of the forms of power of attorney considered later.

In previous times, a power of attorney was an effective – if relatively uncommon – means of providing continuity and certainty where, for example, the granter of the power of attorney was abroad for a prolonged period of time, or else was becoming physically less capable of fully managing their affairs.

In the recent case of *Turner v Turner* [1], Lord Tyre described the role of an attorney in the following terms:-

> "The attorney is thus, in essence, a factor or general and special agent appointed and authorised by the granter to manage his affairs and, in the course of so doing, to bind him in legal relationships with third parties. There is, in my opinion, no legal fiction which treats the attorney as the same person in law as the granter, or which treats the attorney's acts as those of the granter. Rather, the attorney's acts are as valid and binding on the granter as if they had been carried out by him, and the attorney is accountable, as is any

> factor, agent or mandatory, to the granter for his intromissions" [2].

However, at common law, a power of attorney lapsed upon the granter becoming – in the terms of the time – *incapax*. This had the effect of terminating the authority of the attorney, with a consequent uncertainty as to the validity of transactions entered arising arguably at the time the granter was most in need of the facility.

Some progress was made by the enactment of the Law Reform (Miscellaneous Provisions) (Scotland) Act 1990, which overrode the previous common law presumption in relation to the lapsing of any powers of attorney granted after February 1991 [3]. Nevertheless, it was recognised that the extant regime required to be placed on a definitive statutory footing. In particular, any dubiety as to whether powers granted were intended to be of an enduring nature and what would the situation when the granter became "incapable" required to be eliminated [4].

The solution which emerged in the 2000 Act admitted of the creation of two forms of power of attorney; namely, a continuing power of attorney relating to the granter's property and financial affairs, and a welfare power of attorney relating to the granter's personal welfare [5]. Whilst it is not mandatory to grant both forms of power of attorney, as earlier noted, the majority granted will contain both forms, which sometimes is referred to as a mixed power of attorney. While similar in some respects, matters such as supervision of the conduct of the power of attorney will vary [6], as also the powers conferred, a number of statutory requirements are common to both.

In each case, the 2000 Act specifies that in order to be valid, a power of attorney must be signed by its granter. In the case of a continuing power of attorney, the document must "clearly state" that the granter intends the document to be "a continuing power" and in the case of a welfare power of attorney, this must also "clearly state" that a welfare power is intended to be created [7].

Particularly relevant to the subject – matter of this work is how each of the forms of power of attorney comes into effect when an adult loses "capacity". In the case of a continuing power of attorney, it is possible for the authority to become exercisable only upon the event of the granter being "determined to be incapable about the matter to which the power relates" [8].

By contrast, a welfare power of attorney cannot be exercised unless:-

> "(i) the granter is incapable in relation to decisions about the matter to which the welfare power of attorney relates; or
>
> (ii) the welfare attorney reasonably believes that sub-paragraph (i) applies" [9].

Such a provision is commonly termed a "trigger provision".

Consequently, a continuing power of attorney can still be granted and take immediate effect as was the case at common law. More relevant to the present work is how either form of power of attorney can be made effective when – and in the case of a welfare power of attorney, only when – the grantor loses "capacity".

In each case, the document is required to contain a statement that:-

> "if the granter is determined to be incapable in relation to decisions about the matter to which the power relates...the granter has considered how such a determination must be made" (Continuing) [10].
>
> "the granter has considered how a determination as to whether he is incapable in relation decisions about the matter to which the welfare power of attorney related may be made for the purposes [of the test cited above]" [11].

The wording of the legislation leaves open what should comprise the content of the "trigger" but a provision that the issuing of a certificate by a medical practitioner or consultant psychologist that the granter is "incapable", as envisaged by s.1(6) of the 2000 Act [12] is relatively standard. (It also may be prudent to add that verbal advice given to the attorney of the grantor becoming "incapable" will be sufficient for a case of emergency).

In either case, the power of attorney requires to contain a certificate in a prescribed form which is signed by a practising solicitor or member of another prescribed profession [13]. Where a continuing and welfare power of attorney are granted at the same time, it is possible for the process to be covered by a single certificate [14].

Prior to any power of attorney being certified, the certifier must be satisfied that:-

(i) they have interviewed the granter immediately before the granter subscribed the document;

(ii) they are satisfied, either because of their own knowledge of the granter or because they have consulted another person (whom they name in the certificate) who has knowledge of the granter;

(iii) that at the time the continuing power of attorney is granted the granter understands its nature and extent [15].

One possible benchmark is the test set out in *Re K* [16] that a granter could be said to understand the nature and effect of the act conferring the power of authority if they understood:

(a) "that the attorney would be able to assume complete authority over the donor's affairs

(b) that he could do anything with his property that the donor himself could have done (This would be modified in the case of a welfare power of attorney)

(c) that the authority would continue if the donor became mentally incapable

(d) would in that event become irrevocable without confirmation by the Court;

(e) they have no reason to believe that the granter is acting under undue influence or that any other factor vitiates the granting of the power." [17].

The certifier cannot be the person to whom the power of attorney is granted [18]. Guidance issued by the Law Society of Scotland (LSS) expressly states that a solicitor's client is the granter of the power of attorney, and not the granter's relatives, friends or carers. The current professional guidance emphasises the advisability of obtaining expert guidance from a medical practitioner or clinical psychologist in instances of doubt as to a granter's capacity.

The required interview should normally be conducted immediately before signature of the power of attorney by its granter. Seeing the granter alone and consideration of who is the client and the existence of possible conflicts of interest is also advised [19].

The public guardian has stated that certificates signed by a trainee solicitor will be returned, which may imply that a trainee solicitor should not conduct any interview on behalf of the certifier unaccompanied. (The prescribed form of the certificate is set out in Schedule 1 to the Adults with Incapacity (Certificates in Relation to Powers of Attorney) (Scotland) Regulations 2008).

Where the granter is in a hospital or similar facility, it is recommended as good practice for solicitors to make their presence known on the ward, and at least to discuss the granter's capacity with ward staff in cases of doubt. Staff who doubt the granter's capacity, or have concerns regarding coercion or undue influence by a friend or relative, are themselves advised to contact the public guardian [20].

It is important that any concerns regarding the granter's capacity to grant the power of attorney are raised with the public guardian prior to its registration. Once a certificate has been issued by the public guardian, a power of attorney can only be revoked by the Sheriff court [21].

A power of attorney which is not granted in accordance with ss.15 & 16 of the 2000 Act has no effect during the time the granter is incapable in relation to decisions about which the power of attorney relates [22].

Who should be the attorney?

It is competent to appoint a natural or legal person – possibly including a bank or investment company – as a continuing attorney. However, a welfare power of attorney, can only be granted in favour of an individual (which does not include a person acting in their capacity as an officer of a local authority or other body established by or under any enactment) [23].

It is, of course, possible for a continuing and a welfare power of attorney operate in reflection of their separate purposes. It may well be the case, for example, that a granter's solicitor is best placed to manage their property and finances, and a spouse or close relative their personal welfare. Obviously, situations may arise where a decision that benefits the granter's welfare has cost implications, such as in purchasing a replacement car or arranging a community care package.

Joint and substitute attorneys

While there is no overall statistical evidence, it is common for a family member or friend to be granted both continuing and welfare powers of attorney. As mentioned earlier, where difficulties potentially may emerge is when an attorney is also the executor of the granter's will and/or a major beneficiary of that will. In such cases, there will be at best a tension between the two offices, and often an outright conflict of interest arising from the kinds of decisions previously mentioned.

The 2000 Act admits of the possibility of the appointment of one or more joint attorneys, if compatible with the restrictions previously mentioned. Nevertheless, the view of the former public guardian for Scotland is that the potential for dispute between joint attorneys – particularly where relatives are involved – may potentially outweigh the advantage of sharing a significant responsibility [24].

It is correct to acknowledge that difficulties arising in the conduct of a power of attorney may be resolved by obtaining advice from the public guardian [25], or even by seeking directions from the Sheriff Court [26]. There is no established universal solution to such issues, but these highlight the importance of the granter of a power of attorney and the proposed attorney achieving at least a broad understanding of the powers which are to be conferred on the attorney, and obtaining legal advice on possible solutions.

It is also possible to appoint a substitute attorney to act in place of the original appointee. This is not specified in ss.15 & 16 of the 2000 Act, but is referred to in s.23 (4) (b) in circumstances where the original appointee resigns as a continuing and / or welfare attorney [27].

Registering a power of attorney

In order for a continuing or welfare attorney to gain authority to act under a power of attorney, the document must be registered with the public guardian. It is a matter for the discretion of the public guardian whether they are satisfied that the attorney is prepared to act. [28].

Where the public guardian is satisfied that the proposed attorney is prepared to act as such, then prescribed particulars of the document will be entered in the appropriate part of the register maintained by the public guardian [29]. The register is made available for inspection by members of the public during normal office hours [30].

Applications for registration of a power of attorney can be submitted on paper, but the public guardian is also able to accept filing of an application electronically via its EPROAR system. [31]. In cases where giving effect to the power of attorney is required urgently, an expedited procedure is available [32].

A copy of the certificate of registration issued by the public guardian is sent to the sender, and in addition, notice of registration of a welfare power of attorney is also sent to the MWCS and the local authority for the area in which the granter resides [33]. Copies of the welfare power of attorney must be sent by the public guardian to MWCS or the local authority where either so requests [34].

Reference was made above to the inclusion of "trigger" provisions in either a continuing or welfare power of attorney. Such a provision may also specify that the public guardian shall not register the power of attorney until the event specified as activating the "trigger" has occurred.

It will be necessary to notify the public guardian when such an event is considered to have occurred, and the public guardian equally must be satisfied that the event has occurred prior to registering the power of attorney. Again, where the public guardian is not so satisfied, this finding can be appealed to the Sheriff [35].

Where a power of attorney has been registered by the public guardian, the terms of the document, where authenticated by the public guardian:-

> "shall be accepted for all purposes as sufficient evidence of the contents of the original and of any matter relating thereto appearing in the copy" [36].

Despite this confirmation of evidence of the attorney's authority for the purposes of any person with whom the attorney deals, in practice, some bodies – such as banks and building societies – insist on being presented with the original certificate, or else a copy which has been endorsed, whether or not by a solicitor [37]. As this particular document may need time to be returned to the attorney, it is probably advisable to have more than one, and possible several, endorsed copies of the certificate in order to allow operation of the power of attorney to run smoothly and efficiently.

## NOTES (CHAPTER 5)

1. 2012 SLT 877.

2. At Para.12.

3. Law Reform (Miscellaneous Provisions) (Scotland) Act 1990, s.71. The decision of Sheriff Baird in *Application in relation to S* 2013 SLT (Sh. Ct.) 65 suggests that the Courts may be prepared to revise archaic or inadequate provisions contained in older forms of power of attorney, in that case, by interposing a financial guardianship.

4. Scottish Law Commission *Report on Incapable Adults* No 151 (1995), para.3.10.

5. 2000 Act, ss.14(1) (Continuing powers) & 15(1) (Welfare powers).

6. See Chapter 17 below.

7. 2000 Act, ss.15 (3)(b) & 16 (3)(b). Consequently, the 2000 Act refers to the holder of the power of attorney as a "continuing attorney" or "welfare attorney" respectively.

8. 2000 Act., s.15 (3)(ba). The provision must also state that the granter "has considered how such a determination may be made".

9. 2000 Act, s.16 (5)(b).

10. 2000 Act, s.15 (3)(ba).

11. 2000 Act, s.16 (3)(ba).

12. See Chapter 2 above.

13. See the Adults with Incapacity (Certificates in Relation to Powers of Attorney) (Scotland) Regulations 2008, Regn.4. Those authorised to sign a certificate include registered medical practitioners and members of the Faculty of Advocates.

14. 2000 Act, s.16A.

15. 2000 Act, s.15 (3)(c)(ii) (Continuing) & s.16 (3)(c)(ii) (Welfare). At the time of writing, the Scottish Government has proposed that Clinical Psychologists should be added to the list of persons able to certify the capacity of the Granter of a Power of Attorney.

16. [1988] Ch. 310.

17. 2000 Act, ss.15 (3)(c) (iii) (Continuing) & 16 (3)(c)(iii) (Welfare).

18. 2000 Act, ss.15 (4) (Continuing) & 16 (4) (Welfare).

19. LSS *Vulnerable clients* guidance and *guidance on continuing and welfare powers of attorney* (Both May 2022). The MWCS reported a case which illustrated the potential for abuse where a granter did not obtain independent legal advice. (*Report into D* (MWCS) (2012)).

20. *Common concerns about power of attorney* (MWCS) (2020).

21. 2000 Act, s.20 (2)(e). *Common concerns about power of attorney* records the action of a Sheriff who found that a granter of a power of attorney had capacity as at the date of granting, but in the light of concerns regarding the attorney's conduct, made an order placing her under the supervision of the public guardian in financial matters). See also *Public Guardian Applicant 2023 SLT (Sh. Ct.) 133*, for an example of this power being exercised.

22. 2000 Act, s.18.

23. 2000 Act, s.16 (5)(a). The OPG has announced that part of the information recorded when a power of attorney document or an order is registered will include the forename, middle name and surname for each person as stated in the documentation. The legal name will appear on the certificate of registration or appointment.

24. McDonald *Power of attorney: One stop* guide (Kindle) (2021), pp.51-2.

25. 2000 Act, s.6 (2)(e).

26. 2000 Act, s.3 (3).

27. See Chapter 7 below in relation to resignation by an attorney. Appointment of a substitute attorney may be a means of defusing disputes between joint attorneys, but also keeping the power of attorney in operation, where an attorney resigns.

28. In the case of a refusal by the public guardian to register an application, this decision may be appealed to the Sheriff, whose decision is described as being "final" (2000 Act, s.19 (6) (See also Chapter 15 below with regard to a "final" decision of a Sheriff. It was held in *Public Guardian Applicant 2023 SLT (Sh Ct 133*) that a Power of Attorney granted in succession to a previous Power of Attorney which was revoked cannot competently be registered by the Public Guardian where the previous Attorneys have not consented to act as Attorneys. The Scottish Government has proposed that the OPG should be entitled to refuse to Register a Power of Attorney or a Revocation where there is a dispute as to the capacity of the Granter and to call for further Capacity Reports where "reasonable cause" arises.

29. 2000 Act, ss.6 (2)(b)(i) & (ii) & 19 (2)(a). Matters which require to be notified to the public guardian – including the death of the granter or the attorney are set out in 2000 Act, s.23.

30. The public guardian publishes performance against targets on its website in addition to “common reasons for rejection”.

31. 2000 Act, ss.6 (2)(b)(i) & (ii) & 19A (1).

32. The current published target of the public guardian is to register an expedited power of attorney within five working days of a request for expediting. In 2022-23, this was being achieved in 85% of cases.

33. 2000 Act, s.19 (2) (c).

34. 2000 Act, s.19 (5) (c) & (d).

35. 2000 Act, s.19 (3) & (6).

36. 2000 Act, s.19 (4).

37. McDonald, pp.92–3. A style of endorsation of a power of attorney is provided at p.303.

# CHAPTER SIX

# THE TERMS OF A POWER OF ATTORNEY

Beyond containing the mandatory requirements already set out, no form of a power of attorney prescribed by statute. What must be borne in mind is that any power which is not authorised in express terms or by necessary implication in the document runs the risk of being inoperable. While it will ultimately be for the granter to determine the extent of authority they may wish to confer on their attorney, where the point is reached where the granter becomes incapable, it is by then too late to add further powers or modify existing ones.

One simple example of how a continuing and welfare power of attorney might be framed is:-

> Appointment
>
> I, Mary Smith, residing at 24 New Place, Old Town, appoint James Smith, residing at 24 New Place, Old Town and Paul Smith residing at 16 Old Place, New Town to be my continuing attorneys (my "attorney") and each of them alone and the survivor of them in terms of section 15 of the Adults with Incapacity (Scotland) Act 2000 (which act and any subsequent amendment of that is referred to as the "Act").
>
> I appoint the said James Smith and Paul Smith to be my welfare attorneys and each of them alone and the survivor of them as my attorney in terms of section 16 of the Act. My continuing attorneys and my welfare attorneys are each referred to as my attorney.
>
> I declare that I intend that this power of attorney *shall be a continuing and a welfare one* which shall continue to have effect

> even if I shall have lost capacity in relation to the matters in this deed and *I record that I have considered how my incapacity shall be determined for the purposes of this power of attorney* (Emphasis added).
>
> My attorney may manage my whole affairs as my attorney thinks fit and shall have full power for me and in my name or in his/her own name as my attorney to do everything regarding my estate which I could do for myself and that without limitation by reason of anything contained in this power of attorney or otherwise.
>
> In the event of my being incapable in terms of the Act to decisions about my personal welfare, or in the event that *my attorney reasonably believes that that is the case*, then my attorney may make decisions on my behalf in relation to my personal welfare. *I have considered how my incapacity will be determined* (Emphases added).
>
> My attorney shall be subject to the requirements of the Act.
>
> Without prejudice to these general powers my attorney shall have the set powers set out in the following clauses…

This style illustrates how the specific requirements of ss.15 & 16 of the 2000 Act can be met. Firstly, it states that the power granted is a *continuing* power – that is a means of dealing with the contractual and financial affairs of the granter. Secondly, it makes provision that both attorneys have power to deal with such matters. This is important where one or other attorney is unavailable or, as is expressly provided, ensures the power of attorney continues upon the death of one of the attorneys.

What is then set out – and it is not an essential requirement – is provision that the attorney also enjoys powers relating to the welfare of the granter. Examples of the kinds of powers conferred are provided in the *Code of practice for continuing and welfare attorneys* [1] but essentially, it is a matter for the granter to decide, how much or how little authority they wish to relinquish, always bearing in mind that the trigger will be the granter's "incapacity". The mischief to be avoided is, of course, omitting something which neither the incapable granter nor the attorney is able to execute once the power of attorney has been triggered. In some cases, the intention of the granter can be amplified by the incorporation of a statement of will and preferences into the document.

It is possible for the grant of a power of attorney to be drafted so as to provide that the applicable law governing its operation is the law of a state:-

> "(a) of which the granter is a national
>
> (b) in which the granter was habitually resident before the grant
>
> (c) in which the property of the granter is located" [2]

It will be usual to provide that the powers granted to the attorney "shall remain in existence until it is recalled by me or until my death". It is a logical corollary that only a recall executed by a competent granter can terminate a power of an attorney [3]. A continuing power of attorney is also terminated in the event of the bankruptcy of either the granter or the attorney [4].

It is possible, therefore, for a power of attorney to take effect with immediate effect on registration by the public guardian. In the first instance, this will only allow exercise of financial powers where specified in the power of attorney. However, in the situation where the document's provisions – whether financial or welfare – are intended to be triggered only in the event of the adult becoming incapable, the 2000 Act provides that

> "Where the continuing power of attorney is intended *only* if the granter is determined to be incapable...states that the granter has considered *how* such a determination may be made" [5].

It is essential that ss.15 & 16 of the 2000 Act are complied with where applicable to the granting of a power of attorney. Section 18 of the 2000 Act provides that:-

> "shall have no effect during any period when the granter is incapable in relation to decisions about the matter to which the power of attorney relates".

In *B v H* [6], a welfare power of attorney which contained the wording "In the event of my being incapable in terms of the Act in relation to decisions about by personal welfare, or in the event that my attorneys reasonably believe that is the case, then my attorneys may make decisions on my behalf in relation to my personal welfare. I have considered how my incapacity will be determined" was compliant with s.16 (3) (ba) of the 2000 Act, as there was no intention by the granter to state any means [7].

A matter which attracts considerable controversy is whether the voluntary act of the granter of a welfare power of attorney can lawfully authorise the deprivation or restriction of liberty of the granter by their attorney. The issue of deprivation of liberty of an incapable adult is considered at greater length later [8], but recent guidance on the matter is found in the MWCS publication *Common concerns with power of attorney.*

The current view of the MWCS is that a power of attorney cannot authorise a deprivation of liberty. The basis for this view is the absence of protection for an incapable adult who appears to withdraw their consent, where the actual power of attorney must be registered by the public guardian if competent, and potentially capable of being "triggered" without independent verification. Thus, the MWCS recommend either that a welfare guardianship is applied for [9] or directions sought from the Sheriff [10].

Overall, this advice offers a significant caution against assuming that what is potentially a breach of an important convention right can be cured by inserting a carefully worded passage into a welfare power of attorney. The issue goes beyond relations between the granter and welfare attorney and potentially may have a bearing on the lawfulness of actions by members of care and medical staff amongst others.

## NOTES (CHAPTER 6)

1. *Code of practice for continuing and welfare attorneys* (Scottish government) (2018*)*, paras.2.16 & 2.19. The public guardian has also issued *Guidance on the wording in Powers of Attorney: How the Public Guardian will interpret words and phrases* (April 2024). In *Gordon Petitioner 2023 SLT (Sh.Ct 187)*, The terms of a Power of Attorney which authorised an attorney to "raise or defend any actions or judicial or other proceedings in which I am or may be interested so far as my Attorney may consider necessary or expedient" was found to be habile to allow the Attorney of a Widow to be appointed as Executor – Dative in her place where she had become incapax. (c.f. *Cornforth Petitioners2024 SLT (Sh.Ct.) 24*).

2. 2000 Act, Sched.3, para.4(2).

3. See Chapter 7 below.

4. 2000 Act, s.15 (5). The event of bankruptcy on either part does not operate to terminate a welfare power of attorney (2000 Act, s16 (7)).

5. 2000 Act, s.15 (3) (ba) Emphasis added.

6. 2014 SLT (Sh. Ct.) 160.

7. At paras. 34–36 c.f. *Application of Guardianship in respect of* W 2014 SLT (Sh.Ct.) 83. In *Great Stuart Trustees Ltd v Public Guardian* 2015 SLT 115, the Inner House expressed preference for the interpretation given in *B* over *W*.

8. See Chapter 19 below, and reference to cases decided in relation to EConHR, art.5.

9. See Chapter 8 below, and references to *K v Argyll and Bute Council [2021] SAC 2021* which can be viewed as consistent with the

position of MWCS. The public guardian's position is that it is unable to provide advice pending clarification of the law. See FN10 below.

10. *Common Concerns with power of attorney* (MWCS) (2021), paras.10.1 – 2. See also para.18. See however Chapter 24 below, where proposals by the Scottish Government to authorise an Attorney to place the Granter of a Power of Attorney into a deprivation of liberty are considered in more detail.

# CHAPTER SEVEN

# OPERATING A POWER OF ATTORNEY

Financial powers

As noted above, an individual who is appointed as attorney of an adult is subject to compliance with the five principles when exercising any function so arising [1] This consideration is particularly important where operating a power of attorney does not prove to be straightforward.

The *code of practice for continuing and welfare attorneys* ("*the code of* practice") states that:-

> "The attorney may not need to exercise all the powers that you grant. Either the occasion may not arise to exercise particular powers; or he/she may find that when the [five] principles are applied the exercise of the power would not be justified. The important point is that you try to foresee the powers which may be required to meet your needs." [2].

The law and similar guidance generally signal an activist approach by an attorney to the conduct of a power of attorney. In the first instance, this implies that a continuing attorney should have access to adequate, even if not full, information with regard to the granter's financial circumstances.

It is not possible in this work to consider in detail how the five principles might be addressed on a day-to-day basis, but for one example, the obtaining of benefit to the granter might involve moving funds into higher interest accounts. Alternatively, reflecting the granter's previously expressed wishes and feelings may mean eschewing the buying of stocks and shares in favour of national savings certificates. The principle of maximisation of the granter's abilities might be achieved, to give another example, through providing them with a regular allowance to be spent autonomously.

For the reasons previously stated, it will be prudent for the conduct of financial or welfare powers to be kept under a regular review. The *code of practice* generally counsels against being reactive in management of the granter's estate.

This advice connotes remaining aware of recurrent costs of housing, identifying regular outgoings and incomings, being aware of any obligations of aliment or support will be some of the major considerations. The guidance again stresses the availability of specialist advice as well as support from the local authority or public guardian. The need to consider whether obtaining directions from the Sheriff or seeking one of the other orders available under the 2000 Act may offer better outcomes for the granter is also highlighted [3].

It will be particularly important that the will and preferences of the granter – which may be ascertained by various means – are respected as fully as possible by the attorney. Of particular importance may be whether a statement of will and preferences has been adjoined to the power of attorney. Whilst relevant to the conduct of a financial power of attorney, this consideration may be equally significant in the day-to-day conduct of welfare powers, where decisions regarding significant aspects of the granter's lifestyle may be in issue [4].

The guidance of the MWCS is clear that in general, an attorney with welfare powers can seek to persuade the granter to comply with a decision the attorney proposes to make. Ultimately however, the power of attorney cannot oblige compliance with that decision. In such instances, the practicable means of enforcing compliance is obtaining a guardianship order [5].

## What an attorney cannot do

There are several areas where, it is submitted that, however widely or specifically, a power of attorney is drawn, the attorney appointed cannot act. For example, neither a continuing or welfare attorney can be required to anything which would be "unduly burdensome or expensive…having regard to its utility" [6]. There have been no reported cases on this provision, but taken in conjunction with the five principles, an attorney is likely to have a considerable discretion as to when to apply this relief.

Almost certainly, the less benefit likely to accrue to the granter from an action or financial commitment, the easier a decision to decline the step may be. Conversely, something which is likely to bring significant benefit to the granter may mandate the incurring of substantial expense.

A particularly controversial area concerns whether a welfare attorney can authorise admission of the granter to a place where the living conditions amount to a "deprivation of liberty". The view of MWCS is that the law is uncertain in this field, and that a preferable course for an intervention order to be obtained – even where specified in a power of attorney – in order to overcome resistance by an adult to a "significant restriction of liberty" [7]

## The three duties

Whilst not expressly set out in the 2000 Act, the related *Code of practice for continuing and welfare attorneys ("Code of practice")* specifies three duties which apply to anyone who is acting under any form of power of attorney. These are:-

- A fiduciary duty
- A duty of care
- A duty of confidentiality [8].

### (a) Fiduciary duty

Whilst it may seem trite to state that someone placed in a position of trust by the granter of a power of attorney should not act other than in good faith, some content is provided by the *Code of practice* to the effect that:-

> "Decisions must always benefit the granter. Attorneys must not profit or get any personal benefit from their position, apart from receiving gifts where the power of attorney allows it." [9].

It is evident, therefore, that the attorney must always have the interests of the granter at the forefront of any decisions. Clearly, it is also essential that conflicts of interest are avoided where possible [10]. Accordingly, it may be important to consider whether such conflicts are likely to arise when identifying the identity of the attorney or any alternate [11].

Clearly, a power of attorney may be particularly appropriate for allowing a close family member to administer their relative's affairs where he or she loses capacity, but equally this may conflict with other interests such that which an attorney has overall in the estate of the granter, and it is vital that fulfilment of the fiduciary duty is not thus compromised. It is submitted, however, that the fiduciary duty cannot be viewed as going so far as to create an obligation to turn a maximum profit for the granter's estate under a continuing power of attorney.

### (b) Duty of Care

An attorney must act at all times with due skill and care [12]. It would seem axiomatic that a professional attorney would be required to act under reference to professional standards, with a lesser expectation attaching to a lay person. Nevertheless, obtaining professional advice may reasonably be expected of a lay attorney in appropriate circumstances [13].

(c) Duty of confidentiality

An attorney has a duty to maintain confidentiality. [14]. This will include access to the granter's records, use and proper disclosure of confidential information and maintaining the granter's privacy – the latter also being viewed as an aspect of the fiduciary duty. There also is a reciprocal consideration of how far agents of the granter must disclose information in response to the power of attorney, and inclusion of a sufficiently broad authority to obtain such information should be considered in order to avoid disputes.

The former public guardian has outlined in detail some of the considerations relating to the duty of confidentiality, which include:-

- Considering whether the attorney has a legal obligation or duty of confidentiality

- Establishing whether the counterpart has a duty of confidentiality, which may assist the attorney in maintaining their own duty of confidentiality

- Confirming whether the counterpart has a statutory authority to obtain the information [15].

Overall however, the *Code of practice* describes the discharge of the three duties in the following terms:-

> "If you act reasonably and in good faith, and in accordance with the principles, you will not be liable for any breach of any duty of care or fiduciary duty." [16].

Keeping of records

An attorney will is required to keep records of their discharge of their office [17]. While it will be apparent that a setting out of financial transactions entered, and expenditure incurred as attorney, may be the best means of identifying how the estate of a granter has been managed under a continuing power of attorney, recording the conduct of a welfare power of attorney and the basis for decisions being taken which affect the welfare of the granter is equally significant.

## Supervision of attorneys

A continuing attorney is not subject to any express requirement under the 2000 Act to submit accounts to the Sheriff Court, public guardian or other supervisory body. Primarily, any issues in regard to the accuracy or terms of accounts can be raised in initially with the public guardian, who has power to receive and investigate complaints in relation to the exercise of functions relating to the property or financial affairs of an adult made by a continuing attorney [18]. The public guardian is entitled to initiate or take part in any proceedings necessary to protect such interests of an incapable adult [19]

The Sheriff Court also has wide powers of supervision of attorneys, which can be initiated by any person "claiming an interest in the property financial interests or personal welfare" of the granter of a power of attorney [20] and can apply where:-

> "the sheriff is satisfied that the granter is incapable in relation to decisions about, or of acting to safeguard or promote his interests in, his property, financial affairs or personal welfare insofar as the power of attorney relates to them, and that it is necessary to safeguard or promote these interests [21]"

Where the Sheriff determines that this test has been satisfied, a number of orders can be made including requiring the attorney to submit accounts covering a specified period to the public guardian for audit, or to be made subject to the supervision of the public guardian, [22]. The Sheriff also can revoke some of the powers contained in the power of attorney or even revoke the appointment itself. [23].

Overall, a range of mechanisms exist where the conduct of welfare powers by an attorney is questioned. These include:-

- Investigation by the local authority of a complaint [24].
- Exercise of local authority duties under the Adult Support and Protection (Scotland) Act 2007 in relation to an "adult at risk" [25].
- Application to the Sheriff for directions including, for example, requesting the freezing the adult's bank accounts or suspending their income [26].

A welfare attorney is required to provide a local authority with:-

> "any reports or any other information about the personal welfare of the adult or the exercise by the attorney of that attorney's functions as the local authority may reasonably require" [27]

The purpose of such supervision has been described as follows:-

> "amongst the purposes of supervision of welfare attorneys by authorities are....to ensure generally that you are exercising powers in such a way that the person's interests are being safeguarded and promoted. This is important because the person is unlikely to be able to complain effectively if you are not acting appropriately." [28]

The *Code of Practice* further explains aspects of the role as follows:-

> "To assess the impact of any significant changes in circumstances on the person's welfare and the way you carry out your duties as attorney.
>
> To identify any potential need for you to be removed or to have your powers modified.

> To identify if an application should be made for other orders under the Act about the exercise of your powers as welfare attorney. For example, the sheriff may order a welfare attorney to report to him/herself. The sheriff has general powers to make consequential or ancillary orders or directions, impose conditions on orders granted, and call for further information.
>
> To identify whether other measures under the 2000 Act may be necessary, e.g. applications for intervention or guardianship orders". [29].

Again, acceptance of an active role by an attorney is implicit in this guidance. Supervision by the local authority is required only to occur once a month. [30]. Default in the obligation by the local authority may offer a degree of mitigation, but the responsibility for managing the granter's estate and/or welfare properly rests squarely with the attorney. As mentioned above, the relevant guidance sets out the steps open to an attorney who concludes that their current powers are deficient in some manner.

Other practical issues

It may be important to clarify what is best managed via a financial as opposed to a welfare power of attorney. In *Ritchie v Nelson* [31], the granter of a power of attorney had appointed two relatives as her continuing attorney, but a failure to grant welfare powers caused difficulty when the mental state of the granter deteriorated and no member of her family had the power to place her in nursing dementia care [32].

Ending a power of attorney

A power of attorney can be revoked by the granter while competent. Essentially, the process for certification of the grant of a power of attorney [33] requires to be followed in order for the revocation to be effective.

An additional element in this instance is that the certifier requires to be satisfied that "no other factor vitiates the revocation of the power" [34].

A revocation notice has effect when registered by the public guardian, who also amends the public register [35]. A person who acts in good faith in ignorance of the revocation does not incur liability, nor is title to heritable property so acquired challengeable on that ground alone [36].

An attorney is entitled to resign their office by giving notice to the granter, the public guardian, any guardian of the granter, or else their primary carer [37], and also the local authority where a welfare power of attorney is in effect. Notice of resignation does not take effect until 28 days after its receipt by the public guardian, which will result in an amendment to the public register [38].

The 2000 Act seeks to avoid the granter of a power of attorney from being left in a legal vacuum as the result of the resignation of their attorney. Where a joint attorney submits notice of resignation, or where a substitute attorney has been appointed in place of the resigning attorney, the notice does not take effect until the public guardian has evidence that the remaining joint attorney is willing to continue to act, or that the substitute attorney is willing to act [39]. This is not necessarily a straightforward process. (See, for example, *Public Guardian, Applicant* [40], where undue influence on the making of a revocation of a power of attorney by its granter was alleged).

A continuing or welfare power of attorney is terminated in the event that the granter and attorney are married to each other, or in a civil partnership, where decree of separation, divorce or dissolution, or nullity is granted [41]. Authority is similarly terminated on appointment of a guardian "with powers relating to that matter" [42]. No liability attaches to any person acting in good faith in ignorance of the "coming to an end" of a power of attorney by these means, nor can any title to heritable property acquired be challenged on that basis alone [43].

The authority of an attorney acting under a continuing power of attorney ends with the bankruptcy of either the granter or the attorney. By contrast, the same events do not act to end a welfare power of attorney [44].

Cross-border issues

The granting of a power of attorney in Scotland does not guarantee its effectiveness in other parts of the United Kingdom. Banks for example, may have different policies regarding acceptance of the authority of a continuing attorney acting under such powers. The reverse is also true in relation to continuing powers of attorney, where the attorney is described as a financial attorney granted in England.

The public guardian is prepared to issue a certificate of recognition of a foreign power of attorney based on the statement that "interpretation of Scottish legislation [45] suggests a non-Scottish power of attorney is automatically valid in Scotland". The certificate goes on to state that there is no provision got having such a power of attorney endorsed for use in Scotland in the reverse situation, it is possible to apply to the court of protection for a declaration that the power of attorney is recognised and also declared enforceable and registrable in England and Wales [46].

It is also important to clarify as possible where responsibility for operating protective measures lies in cross-jurisdictional circumstances. As drafted, the 2000 Act afforded broad recognition to equivalent measures granted in other jurisdictions, providing that:-

> "Any measure taken under the law of a country other than Scotland for the personal welfare or the protection of property of an adult with incapacity shall, if one of the conditions specified in sub-paragraph (2) is met, be recognised by the law of Scotland" [47]

As examples, in *F v S* [48], a protective order made by French court was considered by a Scottish court to be a measure recognised in Scotland. *In Re O* [49], an incapable adult had moved from England to Scotland, leading to consideration of which was the appropriate forum once a Scottish Court had granted a welfare guardianship, but where the adult's financial attorney had applied to the Court of protection for the adult's return to England.

As the Hague Convention on incapacitated adults was entered into between the twenty signatory States, its effect in the United Kingdom was not changed by the withdrawal of the United Kingdom from the EU in 2019 [50].

## NOTES (CHAPTER 7)

1. See Chapter 2 above. The Scottish Government has proposed that the term "continuing attorney" should be replaced by "financial attorney".

2. *Code of practice for continuing and welfare attorneys* ("*the code of practice*") (Scottish Government) (2018) para.2.17.

3. *Code of practice* paras.4.18, 4.23 & 4.51. See also Chapter 17 below and *Application in respect of D* 2013 GWD 9-205.

4. *Code of practice*, para.1.12. For matters, which might be included in a statement of will and preferences, see *McDonald*, pp.305-312.

5. *Common concerns with power of attorney* (MWCS) (2021), p.9. See Chapter 8 below. It will be apparent from the process outlined there that a matter of some importance would require to arise for the process to be activated. In *G's Guardians v Greater Glasgow Health Board 2021 GWD 40-533*, the Sheriff Appeal Court explicitly stated that the powers invested in a guardian under s.70 of the 2000 Act should not trespass on decisions which as a matter of medical ethics and as a matter of law are clinical judgements (At para.12).

6. 2000 Act, s.17.

7. *MWCS Advice Note, Can a Power of Attorney authorise significant Restrictions of Liberty?* (MWCS) (March 2018). The MWCS also recommend "a proper and auditable process for taking decisions" (*Common Concerns on Power of Attorney*, p13). See also Chapter 6, FN1 above and Chapter 20 below.

8. *Code of practice*, para.3.1. Reference is made to the effect of these duties in later stages of this work. They are of particular relevance in relation to s.82 of the 2000 Act (See Chapter 17 below).

9. *Code of practice*, para.3.1. A recent example of analysis of the fiduciary duty of an Attorney can be found in *Kaye's Executor Nominate v Kaye's Former Attorney 2023 SLT 589.* (See also Chapter 17 below)

10. *Code of practice*, paras.4.47 – 49.

11. See Chapter 5 above.

12. *Code of practice*, para.4.18 (Continuing), para.5.15 (Welfare).

13. *Code of practice*, para.4.27.

14. *Code of practice*, para.3.1.

15. *Code of practice*, para.3.2. See McDonald, p.264.

16. *Code of practice*, para.3.2.

17. 2000 Act, s.21. The use of Records kept by an Attorney in an Action of Count, Reckoning and Payment was considered in *Campbell v Campbell's Exx 2021 CSOH 3.*

18. 2000 Act, s.6 (3)(c)(i).

19. 2000 Act, s.6 (2) (a).

20. 2000 Act, s.20 (1).

21. 2000 Act, s.20 (2).

22. 2000 Act, s.20 (2) (a) & (b). Decisions of the Sheriff made in terms of s.20 (2) (a) – (d) are stated to be "final" (s.20 (4)). See Chapter 15 below. The Scottish Government has proposed that the OPG should obtain powers to place an Attorney under Supervision; to give an Attorney Directions and to suspend an Attorney, subject in each case to a right of Appeal to the Sheriff.

23. 2000 Act, s.20 (e).

24. 2000 Act, s.10 (1) (c)(i).

25. See Chapter 22 below.

26. 2000 Act, s.3 (3).

27. Adults with Incapacity (Supervision of Welfare Attorneys by Local Authorities) (Scotland) Regulations 2001, regn.3.

28. *Code of practice*, para.5.70.

29. *Code of practice*, para.5.71.

30. 2001 Regulations, regn.2 (1).

31. 2016 CSOH 35.

32. At para.82. The case itself concerned the validity of a disposition granted by an adult, and no issue of how a lack of power to place the adult into nursing care could have been cured was addressed, as she had by then died.

33. 2000 Act, s.22. See Chapter 5 above.

34. 2000 Act, s.22A (2)(iii).

35. 2000 Act, s.22A (3).

36. 2000 Act, s.22A (5). See Chapter 19 below.

37. 2000 Act, s.23 (1).

38. 2000 Act, s.23 (2).

39. 2000 Act, s.23 (4). A Power of Attorney granted in succession to a previous Power of Attorney which was revoked cannot

competently be registered by the Public Guardian where the previous Attorneys have not consented to act as Attorneys (*Public Guardian Applicant 2023 SLT (Sh Ct 133*).

40. 2011 SLT (Sh.Ct.) 66.

41. 2000 Act, s.24 (1) & (1A).

42. 2000 Act, s.24 (2).

43. 2000 Act, s.24 (4). See Chapter 19 below.

44. 2000 Act, s.15 (5) (Continuing) & s.16 (7) (Welfare).

45. That is the 2000 Act.

46. Public guardian website.

47. 2000 Act, schd.3, para.7 (1). A number of exceptions to this broad rule are set out in para 7(3).

48. 2012 SLT (Sh.Ct.) 189.

49. [2014] Fam 197.

50. A statement in a previous edition of this work to the effect that the operation of the Hague Convention had become uncertain as the result of the United Kingdom leaving the European Union was erroneous. In any event, the registration of intra-UK judgements in terms of the Civil Jurisdiction and Judgements Act 1982, schd.7 also continued unaffected.

# CHAPTER EIGHT

# GUARDIANSHIP ORDERS

One colourable analysis of a guardianship order when viewed against the five statutory principles, is that it is "the most restrictive option" of an adult's freedom available under the 2000 Act. As will be seen, the extent of legal capacity which a guardianship order can remove from an adult can be comprehensive.

In cases such as a major traumatic brain injury or persistent vegetative state (PVS), there may be little in the way of capacity remaining for an adult to exercise. However, even in such serious or extreme cases, the adult may have expressed views or wishes prior to losing their capacity. One protection the 2000 Act offers is the principle of taking such views into account where decisions are made [1].

However, it is questionable whether the granting of a guardianship order can be viewed solely through the prism of the five principles. As will be considered later, the operation of the EConHR, and particularly art.5 (Deprivation of liberty), art.8 (Right to family and private life) and art.14 (Non – discrimination in enjoyment of Convention rights) and also arts.12,19, 20 and 23 of the CRPD) are potentially relevant also [2].

However, the purpose of the process of appointing a guardian is summarised in the *Code of Practice for persons authorised under intervention orders and guardians* [3] as mandating a formal assessment of

- The adult's capacity [4]
- Checks on the suitability of the proposed guardian [5]
- Registration of the appointment with the public guardian [6]

Where does the jurisdiction of the Sheriff Court arise?

Both judicial and administrative authorities [7] have jurisdiction under the 2000 Act where:

"(a) the adult is habitually resident in Scotland; or

(b) property which is the subject of the application or proceedings or in respect of which functions are carried out under [the 2000 Act] is in Scotland; or

(c) the adult, although not habitually resident in Scotland is there or property belonging to the adult is there and, in either case, it is a matter of urgency that the application is or the proceedings are, dealt with; or

(d) the adult is present in Scotland and the intervention sought in the application or proceedings is of a temporary nature and its effect limited to Scotland." [8].

Within Scotland, jurisdiction is defined as follows:-

> "The sheriff having jurisdiction under this schedule to take measures is the sheriff in whose sheriffdom—
>
> (a) in relation to a case falling within paragraph 1(1)(a), the adult is habitually resident;
>
> (b) in relation to a case falling within paragraph 1(1)(b), the property is located;
>
> (c) in relation to a case falling within paragraph 1(1)(c), the adult or property belonging to the adult is present;
>
> (d) in relation to a case falling within paragraph 1(1)(d), the adult is present." [9]

One further relevant provision is that:-

> "Notwithstanding that any other judicial or administrative authority has jurisdiction, a sheriff shall have jurisdiction to take measures if:-
>
> "(a) the adult is present in the sheriffdom;
>
> (b) the sheriff considers that it is necessary, in the interests of the adult, to take the measures immediately" [10]

What is "habitual residence"?

In broad terms, assessment of "habitual residence" is a matter of fact and not law and will embrace numerous factors, which may establish the degree of integration of a person in a social and family environment [11]. It is important to consider this issue prior to seeking a guardianship order, notwithstanding that "habitual residence" is a term which has a general recognition in law [12].

In the case of *DB (A Patient)*, two Scottish adults who had resided continually in an English hospital for 6 or 7 years, but who intended to return to family in Scotland – even then living in a residential unit – were held by the English Court of protection to have gained a habitual residence in England [13]. By contrast, in *Darlington BC, Applicants* [14], Sheriff Mackie concluded that where the Court of protection had sanctioned the move of an adult from an English care home to a Scottish care home for a six-week trial period, this did not disturb the adult's habitual residence in England [15].

<u>Who can apply for a Guardianship order?</u>

A very wide definition of who is entitled to apply for a guardianship order is applied by the 2000 Act, which authorises an application by:-

> "any person (including the adult his/herself) claiming an interest in the property, financial affairs or personal welfare of [the] adult" [16]

While this provides a pathway to persons such as a relative, carer, friend or professional to apply, where:-

> "no application has been made, or is likely to be made"

and an guardianship order is:-

> "necessary for the protection of the adult's property, financial affairs or personal welfare."

the local authority in which the adult resides is required to apply for a guardianship order where no other application has been made, or is likely to be made, in relation to an adult who satisfies the conditions for making the order [17].

In *J Solicitor, Applicant* [18], a solicitor sought guardianship powers in relation to an 84 year old woman who had suffered a stroke. The Sheriff at first instance held that an interest as the adult's solicitor did not amount to an "interest in the financial affairs" of the adult. The solicitor did not hold any power of attorney for his client. The right of the adult to have a suitable and qualified guardian was held not to have been compromised, given the obligation of the local authority to apply for such an appointment.

On appeal, the Sheriff Principal observed that:-

> "The 2000 Act provides a statutory code to meet the needs of adults who lack full legal capacity. Indeed, it can be said that an adult lacking capacity has a right to a suitable and qualified guardian. Accordingly, this is no ordinary litigation seeking to convene a defender to court, instead the object of the application

is solely to address the needs of the adult in question and determine the proper form of intervention in the adult's affairs." [19].

In the event, the Sheriff's decision was not reversed on the basis that the appeal itself was incompetent, but also that there were no circumstances requiring intervention to protect the needs and interests of the adult, standing the duties imposed on the local authority by the 2000 Act [20] What can be taken from this decision is that suitability of an applicant does not necessarily equate with sufficient interest.

Support for an application may be available is available from either Legal advice and assistance (LAA) or Legal aid if an application is to be made for a guardianship order or intervention order containing welfare or welfare and financial powers. LAA will be awarded based upon the resources of the adult and not the applicant, in order to apply the test of financial eligibility

Legal aid will be awarded without a means test in cases where an application for a guardianship order seeks welfare powers. Where no welfare powers are sought, eligibility will be assessed on the basis of the adult's resources [21].

The functions of a guardian

There are several key criteria on which anyone wishing to be appointed as a guardian requires to satisfy the Sheriff. These are that the applicant:-

(a) is aware of the adult's circumstances and condition, and of the needs arising from such circumstances and condition

(b) is aware of the functions of a guardian. [22].

Moreover, the Sheriff is directed to have regard to:-

i) the applicant's accessibility to the adult and their primary carer (if any)

ii) their ability to carry out the functions of a guardian

iii) any likely conflict of interest between the applicant and the adult

iv) any undue concentration of power which is likely to arise in the individual over the adult

v) any adverse effects which the appointment of the individual would have on the interests of the adult

vi) such other matters which appear appropriate to the Sheriff [23].

It will be noted that the process of judicial authorisation of a guardianship order, creates a number of safeguards which the granter of a power of attorney does not necessarily require to address. Nevertheless, there are relatively few reported decisions regarding the operation of s.59 (3) of the 2000 Act, and in almost every instance, the Sheriff requires to address a fact specific situation.

One example of consideration of some of the factors attending an "undue concentration of power" is *West Lothian Council, Applicant* [24], where the local authority was appointed as guardian to an adult in preference to her son, whose hostility to the local authority and unwillingness to accept the views and advice of others was found, aligned with a breach of an express condition not to use physical chastisement, to have created both a conflict of interest, as well as risk an undue concentration of power in the son [25].

Aside from what is set out in the averments regarding the suitability of the proposed guardian, it is submitted that the Sheriff will always have regard to the five principles and the report submitted by the MHO [26], as also to the relevant medical evidence.

It will be appreciated that such considerations are underpinned by concerns of providing benefit to the adult from the guardianship. Thus, refusal of an application on one or more of the grounds is not necessarily a comment on the morality or motivation of the proposed guardian. The exercise at this point is one of satisfying the Court that the guardianship can be operated effectively, and that the proposed guardian is not taking an over-optimistic view of their ability to discharge the office.

Clearly, the latter criteria also contain a protective element. The Court must be reasonably assured that the prospective guardian will not be influenced by personal considerations in any actions they take, or worse, become an overbearing influence in the adult's life.

This can beg the question of whether close family members can properly discharge the role. A son or daughter is highly likely to have some interest in inheriting from their parent and concerned by potential dissipation of assets. On the other hand, the adult may have very few other relations outwith their immediate family circle.

Accordingly, a balance must be struck between the potential risks and benefits of a specific applicant. The Sheriff, of course, has the option of hearing from the applicant and any other witnesses, particularly if the MHO's report has raised any concerns, and there also are supervisory powers available to statutory officers with a view to preventing abuse from arising in any form [27].

Overall, s.59 of the 2000 Act should be regarded as investing the Sheriff with a wide discretion in applying its terms, in conjunction with the five principles, to the facts of any instant application. On the basis of the decision of SP Stephen in *G v West Lothian Council* [28], a higher Court is unlikely to disturb the outcome of such an exercise unless the decision can be shown to be "plainly wrong" [29]. In this case, a challenge to the appointment of the CWSO as interim guardian to an elderly woman, following concerns regarding the previous exercise of welfare powers by her son, was upheld.

## Is the Adult incapable?

Whilst ultimately the matter requires to be determined by the Sheriff, the capacity of any adult subject to an application for a guardianship order is likely to be a medical issue primarily. However, it is important to recall that the question cannot simply be reduced to a pass/fail form of analysis.

Certainly, two medical practitioners may agree that an adult has lost capacity, but may dispute the extent to which that has occurred. In some cases, the issue of whether capacity has been lost at all may be the source of disagreement. Recently, the Scottish Government has consulted on whether to widen the scope of professionals who can properly certify incapacity [30].

Most non-statutory guidance refers to the definition of "incapacity" set out in s.1(6) of the 2000 Act. On a broad view, this may offer something of a yardstick, but a close reading of the legislation and the five principles implies that the focus properly should be on the decision(s) the adult is unable to take; the existence of a need to take one or more of these; and whether an "intervention" is necessary. Such an analysis appears to sit more closely with the approach of minimum intervention adopted in the 2000 Act.

It is an oversimplification therefore, to regard medical opinion as being necessarily conclusive of an adult's incapacity as a matter of law. As will be seen, a specific path is established for a MHO, a qualified social worker with a specialist accreditation in mental health and capacity matters, to provide information of their assessment of the adult, and also to state whether they are supportive or otherwise of the application for guardianship.

Beyond that however, reference will also be made to the range of persons who require to be notified of a guardianship application, including, as previously mentioned, "anyone having [an interest] in the property, welfare and interests" of the adult. Accordingly, a range of views may be available to the Sheriff regarding the extent of an adult's capacity, including of course, those of the adult him or herself.

What factors should be taken into account?

One suggested set of matters which may require to be balanced in the process include:-

- Understanding of the nature of a decision, act or transaction
- Where a series of linked decisions is required, and understanding of each element and their interrelationship
- Where choices require to be made, an understanding of the nature of those choices and the ability to evaluate them
- Where choices are present, the ability to add further relevant options which have not been presented
- Knowledge of relevant circumstances, and understanding of their relevance;
- The ability to retain the foregoing long enough to make a decision (or a coherent series of decisions)
- Where a decision has been requested, ability to recognise when such a decision may not be necessary, or immediately necessary), and ability to decline to make it (or to defer it) in such circumstances the ability to make, and to commit to, a decision
- Ability to communicate the decision
- Ability to retain memory of the decision for an appropriate period" [31].

The centrality of considering the needs and ability of any adult who may become subject to an application for a guardianship order closely and in an individual manner cannot be overstated. Taken together, the five principles point strongly against seeking an all – embracing assumption of legal agency from a person whose current or future capacity does not require such a course to be taken. Formulation of an application, therefore, always should be viewed as a careful and discerning process.

It is important to appreciate that any authority to provide medical treatment to an adult in terms of s.47 (2) of the 2000 Act is essentially frozen pending determination of an application for a guardianship or intervention order, until it is finally determined unless authorised by "any other enactment or rule of law for the preservation of the life of the adult or the prevention of serious deterioration in their medical condition [32].

## NOTES (CHAPTER 8)

1. 2000 Act, s.1(4) – See Chapter 3 above.

2. See Chapter 24 below.

3. For the purposes of Chapters 7-15, "the *code of practice*".

4. See Chapter 2 above.

5. *Code of practice*, paras.4.42-44.

6. *Code of Practice*, paras.4.34-46. Similar considerations inform the appointment of an intervener or withdrawer (See Chapters 14 & 16 below).

7. The public guardian, MWCS, local authorities and "supervisory bodies" (see Chapter 17 below) (2000 Act, Sched.3, para.14).

8. 2000 Act, Sched.3, para.1. Schedule 3 of the 2000 Act reflects the Hague convention of 13th January 2000 on protection of adults. This may have a bearing on the operation of the Act of Sederunt (Summary Applications, Statutory Applications and Appeals Etc.) Rules 1999, Part XXIV, which deals with the international protection of adults.

9. 2000 Act, Sched 3, para.2 (1).

10. 2000 Act, Sched. 3, para. 2 (3). In certain circumstances, the Sheriff of Lothian and Borders at Edinburgh will have jurisdiction by default (2000 Act, Sched.3, para.2 (4)).

11. *A v A* [2013] UKSC 60, at para.54. In *FT v MM* [2019] EWHC 953 (Fam), the Court observed that "habitual residence" is to be assessed by reference to all the circumstances as they exist at the time of assessment (at para.13). Accordingly, the cases referred to offer only limited guidance to the outcome of a specific

determination of an adult's "habitual residence" (See also FN 15 below).

12. *DB (A Patient)* [2016] EWCOP 30.

13. At paras. 33-36.

14. 2018 SLT (Sh.Ct.) 53.

15. *DB* at para.54. A previously recognised test provided in *R v Barnet LBC ex.p. Shah* [1983] 2 AC 309 was expressly disapproved by the UK Supreme Court in *A v A (Children) (Habitual Residence)* [2014] AC 1. Inherently, the "habitual residence" of an adult is fact specific, and recently, a list of established criteria was set out in the decision of Moylan J in *The Health Service Executive of Ireland v IM and Anr [2020] EWCOP 51 (at para.39) (c.f. Aberdeenshire Council v SF [2023] EWCOP 28 at para.16).*

16. 2000 Act, s.57 (1). It has not been determined whether the approach adopted in *B Minuter 2014 SLT (Sh. Ct) 5* (See Chapter 3 above) is equally applicable in qualifying to apply for a guardianship order.

17. 2000 Act, s.57 (2).

18. [2016] SC EDIN 66.

19. Per SP Stephen at para.13.

20. At para.15.

21. *Code of practice*, para.1.24. For the current Guidance on awards of Legal Aid by SLAB in guardianship cases, see https://www.slab.org.uk/guidance/adults-with-incapacity-awi/.

22. 2000 Act, s.59 (3).

23. 2000 Act s.59 (4). A conflict of interest or apparent undue concentration of power do not relate to an applicant by reason only that they are a "close relative" or person residing with the adult (2000 Act, s.59 (5)). It is submitted, however, that these matters remain relevant considerations for the Sheriff to consider overall.

24. 2015 GWD 12-219.

25. See the Sheriff's analysis at paras.99 – 107.

26. See Chapter 9 below.

27. See Chapter 17 below.

28. 2014 GWD 40 -730.

29. At paras.24 & 38.

30. *Consultation on the adults with incapacity (Scotland) Act 2000* (Scottish Government) (2018), Chapter Six. The Scottish Government has proposed that Clinical Psychologists are added to the list of persons authorised to provide reports on a Adult's capacity.

31. Adrian Ward, *Mental Incapacity*, (SULI) (2003), para.1-30.

32. 2000 Act, s.49 (1) & (2). Any authority obtained cannot overbear an Interdict prohibiting the provision of such medical treatment (subs.(3)). See Chapter 23 below.

# CHAPTER NINE

# OBTAINING A GUARDIANSHIP ORDER

What is required to accompany a guardianship application?

It may be apparent at this stage that a range of factors may require to be present in order to support an application for guardianship successfully, and it is important to consider these from an early stage in that process. The Sheriff Court can be asked – as is the case for powers of attorney – to make a guardianship order in relation to an adult's property and financial affairs, their welfare, or both [1].

In practice, the vast majority of guardianship orders granted will provide both financial and welfare powers [2]. However, keeping the five principles in mind, an applicant for such an order should address at an early stage whether the application should seek both forms of powers, and why this is necessary and appropriate for the adult.

Medical evidence

Another important matter requiring early consideration is the obtaining of medical reports in support of a guardianship application. The 2000 Act requires the provision of two reports, in a prescribed form [3]. The reports must record the outcome of a medical examination and assessment of the adult carried out by a medical practitioner not more than 30 days before the application is lodged [4]. Where the Sheriff is satisfied that there has been no change in circumstances since an examination and assessment was made, the Court may consider an application where this occurred more than 30 days before the lodging of the application. [5]

Where the incapacity arises by reason of mental disorder, one of the reports requires to be written by a "relevant medical practitioner" [6].

Financial guardianship

Where financial powers only are to be sought, the guardianship application must be accompanied by a report, in a prescribed form, "by a person who has sufficient knowledge to make such a report" regarding:-

(i) the general appropriateness of the order sought, based on an interview and assessment of the adult carried out not more than 30 days before the lodging of the application; and

(ii) the suitability of the individual nominated in the application to be appointed guardian [7]

The assessment of the suitability of the proposed guardian conducted by the author of the report should have regard to both the criteria the Sheriff is required to consider, as well as the five principles [8]. The author is also required to seek the wishes and feelings of the adult and the views of the adult's nearest relative, primary carer and any guardian, continuing attorney, welfare attorney or "any relevant person" [9].

Welfare guardianship

Where the application embraces a welfare guardianship, it requires to be accompanied by a report in a prescribed form, completed by an MHO [10]. As with other reports, the report prepared by the MHO must be based on an interview and assessment of the adult carried out not more than 30 days before the lodging of the application [11].

Again, the MHO requires to ascertain the wishes and feelings of the adult, and to obtain the views of the adult's nearest relative, primary carer and any guardian, continuing attorney, welfare attorney or "any other relevant person". Additionally, the MHO is required to assess the appropriateness of the order sought and the suitability of the proposed guardian on the same basis as applied to the financial powers report [12].

Similarly, the prescribed form of the MHO report contains a section on declaration of interest. A significant analysis of whether any professional interest created conflict or bias on the part of an MHO was made in *Aberdeenshire Council v JM* [13]. There, the overall purpose of the MHO's report was held to be one of obtaining their opinion as to the appropriateness of the order sought, based on their interview with the adult and their assessment of the adult. Equally important is the assessment of the proposed guardian [14].

Practical considerations

It is important to appreciate that in order for an application for a guardianship order to be made validly, a number of items need to be assembled within a relatively short period of time, but also in compliance with specified time limits. It is advisable therefore, to carry out as much advance planning as can reasonably be achieved.

Nevertheless, assembling the required reports within these time limits may be no simple task. While the starting point for the medical examinations and reports may be the adult's GP – who may be the person who discovered a possible loss of capacity initially – some other suitably qualified medical practitioner will require to be identified to conduct a counterpart examination.

In practice, even greater issues may attend the preparation of the MHO report. It will be seen that a number of people may need to be interviewed by the MHO, including the adult. It cannot be ignored that for a number of years recently, a shortage of MHOs has been experienced. Also, it should not be forgotten that MHOs also discharge responsibilities under the 2003 Act, alongside of a high or increasing level of guardianship work.

Consideration must also be given to what documentation should accompany an application. The initiating writ for a guardianship application is a summary application. Accordingly, the procedure is governed by the Act of Sederunt (Summary Applications, Statutory Applications and Appeals etc) Rules 1999, rr.3.16.1 – 13 ("the SAR"). The wording set out as Form 23 of the SAR itself prescribes little specific detail for inclusion within the summary application

However, it already has been seen that a significant amount of information will require to be presented to the Court in support of the application. Some content to what may be required is provided in a detailed practice note which was issued in updated form by the Sheriff Principal of Lothian and Borders in 2024. The document itself is not reproduced in full here, but amongst important requirements set out are:-

> "(a) All craves of the application seeking powers in relation to an adult must specify the full name, as well as any other name by which the adult is known, current address, and date of birth of the adult.
>
> "(b) Where application is made for the grant of both (1) welfare powers and (2) property and/or financial powers, these must be grouped separately from each other. Proposed powers should be listed with numbers or letters and not bullet points.
>
> (c) If an application seeks the appointment of a substitute guardian, the crave should (1) specify that this is to be in the event of death, incapacity or resignation of the original guardian, and (2) set out in full the proposed powers sought to be conferred on the proposed substitute guardian, in a separate crave or craves as appropriate.
>
> "(d) The crave or craves in a minute for renewal should set out in full the powers sought to be renewed.
>
> "(e) Where an application seeks powers in relation to heritable property, a full postal address is required. It should contain within

> the crave the title number in the Land Register for Scotland, failing which a full conveyancing description sufficient to identify the property in the Register of Sasines."

The Practice Note now specifies that to assist with the efficient and accurate production of interlocutors, applicants who are represented are required to produce a complete draft interlocutor to the court in advance of the hearing. Where changes to the craves have been suggested by the sheriff or safeguarder and accepted by the applicant, these must be incorporated.

Information is required as to whether any proposed appointee has been barred from working with vulnerable adults or been convicted of a criminal offence, and if so, full details must be specified.

The writ must include averments setting out accurately:-

(1) the full name, address and designation and relationship to the adult of the adult's nearest relative;

(2) the full name, address and designation of the adult's primary carer;

(3) the full name, address and designation of the adult's named person (if any);

(4) the full name, address and designation of any guardian, continuing attorney or welfare attorney of the adult who has any power relating to the application or proceedings [15];

(5) the full name, address and designation of any other person who may have an interest in the application and, if the adult has a number of children or siblings to be specified, specifying them in order of age starting with the oldest;

(6) If the whereabouts of the nearest relative or any named person are not known and cannot reasonably be ascertained, the writ

must contain averments setting out the steps which have been taken to trace the nearest relative and/or named person concerned. Furthermore, if there is no known nearest relative or named person, the writ must contain averments to that effect;

(7) The writ must also include a schedule listing (with numbers or letters and not with bullet-points) the full names, addresses and designations of all those on whom intimation of the application is sought, including the public guardian, the MWCS (where appropriate) and the relevant local authority (where appropriate);

(8) If the adult is in an "authorised establishment" the writ must include averments to this effect and include the full name and address of the establishment together with any known details about the managers of that establishment [16];

(9) The writ must contain averments as to the known existence or otherwise of any existing power of attorney granted by the adult. The writ must include averments as to the present and past wishes and feelings of the adult about the order sought and the powers requested so far as they can be ascertained. If it is not possible to ascertain them, the writ must include averments (a) as to why this is not possible and (b) as to the steps taken, if any, (including any assistance and/or support provided) with a view to ascertaining them.

(10) Where application is being made for the grant of property and/or financial powers, the application must contain details of the extent and current value, if known, of all heritable and moveable property belonging to the adult.

(11) Where interim powers or orders are being sought, the application must contain averments specifying the reasons therefor. In addition, if a hearing on the crave for interim powers or orders is sought prior to the principal hearing assigned, the applicant should make clear in a covering letter to the court

which powers are sought ad interim and setting out reasons for any perceived urgency.

(12) Where application is being made for the appointment of joint guardians, the application must contain averments which satisfy the requirements of section 62(2) of the 2000 Act; or enable the court to be so satisfied.

(13) Applicants, (including those who are making counter-proposals for appointment by way of craves made in answers), are reminded that to enable the sheriff to determine whether an individual is suitable for appointment as guardian (including substitute, additional or replacement guardians), supporting material requires to be lodged. In addition, except in cases where the application solely seeks appointment of the chief social work officer of a local authority, the application (and accompanying reports) must contain such details as to the character, background, and any relevant financial or investment experience of, any person whose appointment is sought as a guardian (including a substitute, additional or replacement guardian) or intervener, accompanied by such letters of reference as may be considered appropriate or which may be required by the court, in order that the court can determine suitability for appointment. Proposed financial guardians should complete the Guardian Declaration Form and lodge this with the application; and for this to be intimated to the OPG with the application after warrant.

(14) Except in cases where the application solely seeks appointment of the chief social work officer of a local authority, the application must be accompanied by a letter from each person whose appointment is sought as a guardian (including substitute, additional or replacement guardian) or intervener, specifying whether or not he or she has at any time (a) been barred from working with vulnerable adults, or (b) been convicted of a criminal offence in Scotland or elsewhere and, if so, providing

full details thereof for consideration by the court prior to warranting.

(15) Where application is being made for the grant of property and/or financial powers, the application must contain averments as to whether or not any proposed financial guardian (including substitute, additional or replacement guardian) or intervener (1) is or has ever been sequestrated or been made subject to a bankruptcy restriction order; (2) has ever signed a trust deed for creditors; (3) is or ever has been subject to or applied for a debt payment programme; (4) is or has ever been subject to an order pursuant to the Company Directors Disqualification Act 1986; (5) is or ever has been subject to an inhibition or arrestment, or has been made subject to any similar order or taken such similar steps in Scotland or elsewhere and, if so, to include details thereof.

(16) The duration of any order sought and the basis of any award of expenses sought should be dealt with in the application and a crave or craves in appropriate terms included. If there is a legal aid certificate, this should be made clear.

(17) Where application is being made for powers in relation to property and/or financial affairs the default is for caution to be found with a crave for the amount sought and details set out in the application. Where it is proposed to dispense with caution reasons require to be stated in the application to enable the court to consider the request.

(18) Where the application is for the appointment of a solicitor as financial guardian or substitute, additional or replacement financial guardian, the report as to the suitability of the solicitor nominated to be so appointed, and as to the general appropriateness of the order sought must be from a person who is not a partner, employer, consultant, associate, employee or fellow employee of the solicitor. [17].

Prior to lodging the application, consideration should be given to whether the Court should be asked to dispense with service of the application on the adult. The SAR require submission of two certificates, issued by medical practitioners independent of each other, stating that intimation of the application or other proceeding, or relative interlocutor, would be "likely to pose a serious risk to the health of the adult" [18]. One of the two medical practitioners must be an approved medical practitioner for the purposes of the 2003 Act [19].

It is submitted that a reasoned justification for such a request warrants some thought. The adult in question has not at this stage been judicially determined to be incapable. Moreover, the terms of the five principles and the ECHR and CRPD also imply that good reason should be established for excluding the adult from any part of judicial proceedings directly affecting them. How far should the possibility of distress or harm be relied upon? The assent of the Sheriff to dispensing with intimation to the adult should not be presumed, therefore [20].

Another important matter to keep in mind also is whether exercise of the power of the Court to grant interim orders or give directions should be sought. It is possible to seek the appointment of an interim guardian at any point prior to determination of the guardianship application itself [21], and such an application can be made by inclusion of an appropriate crave in the application, or by motion at a later point [22].

Again, the effect of such orders or directions may have a significant impact on the adult, as it can effectively divest the adult of some or all of their ability to act before matters such as the adult's incapacity, or the extent of it have been judicially determined. There are a number of considerations to be balanced, and it is submitted that a strong level of necessity for granting an interim order in order to protect the adult's welfare and / or their property from imminent or substantial harm must be demonstrated, in order to comply with the five principles.

If financial guardianship is being sought, then consideration to how caution can be arranged will also require to precede the application [23].

It will be apparent that the powers which the Court is being asked to grant to the guardian require to be justified, and must be carefully considered. The principle of minimum intervention appears to place the burden on the applicant to make the running. Are the powers being too widely drawn? Alternatively, will what is sought be sufficient to cover foreseeable eventualities?

Possible areas which might be addressed in an application for guardianship may include the following:-

Powers Craved

- Power to manage the property and financial affairs of the adult
- Power to carry out transactions or categories of transactions
- Power to carry out specific transactions (It is appropriate to specify a conveyancing description or title number for any heritable property) [24]
- Power to deal with specified aspects of the adult's welfare
- Period over which the powers should be exercised [25]
- Expenses of the application should be sought from the adult's estate [26].

Statements of fact

- An explanation of the benefit to accruing to the adult from the application and how development of the adult's capacity and skills might be encouraged.
- Explanation of why benefit cannot be achieved without the powers as sought.

- Justification for any extended period of the guardianship order [27].

- Why the prospective guardian is suitable for appointment.

- How many people might hold the office of guardian at the time of making the application or in the future [28].

In the case of financial guardianship, relevant matters might include:-

- Power to manage the property and financial affairs of the adult

- Power to carry out transactions or categories of transactions to be conducted

- Power to carry out specific transactions (if so, it is necessary to append a sufficient conveyancing description of any heritable property which may form part of the guardianship order)

In the case of an application for welfare guardianship, which aspects of the adult's welfare anticipated to receive benefit may need to be specified in some detail.

The period of the guardianship sought should be set out, if longer than the default period of 3 years [29].

One important procedural matter clarified in *Aberdeenshire Council v JM* [30] is that a counter – proposal of who should be appointed as a guardian is not a "subsequent application" requiring to be made by minute [31].

It should be apparent, therefore, that preparation of an application for a guardianship order essentially mandates the need to work backwards from the intended date of lodging the application to ensure that:-

(a) Examinations will be sufficiently proximate.

(b) Whether intimation of the application should be dispensed with as regards the adult has been considered [32].

(c) Other required supporting documentation will be gathered.

(d) What may require to happen, pending determination of the application (Interim guardianship and/ or directions)

(e) Whether caution can be arranged (This is only required if seeking financial guardianship) [33].

(f) Where financial powers are sought, will a management plan require to be prepared? Should permission to dispense with a management plan be sought from the Sheriff and the public guardian? [34].

(g) Should the local authority / public guardian (Financial) / MWCS (Welfare) be consulted?

(h) Is the local authority providing community care services which would "help the adult to benefit from the service"? [34].

(i) Could a different form of regulation be applied? What alternatives have been considered and rejected?

(j) Do any conflicts of interest arise?

Expenses of the application should be sought from the estate of the adult.

A very brief heading of the relevant statements of fact is prescribed in the SAR, Form 23.

Further additional required information is likely to include:

(a) Specification of the adult's condition and any prognosis for the future

(b) Explanation of the benefit likely to accrue to the adult and why that cannot be achieved without the powers being sought

(c) Justification of any extended period of guardianship being sought; in effect why it is unnecessary for the order to require to be renewed after 3 years, and possibly at all

If the summary application is accepted, the Court will fix a hearing in the normal way by issuing an interlocutor, and order intimation and the lodging of answers in a specified period [35] Given the number of persons who require to be consulted in the preparation of reports supporting the application [36], the number of persons for whom the scope of intimation of the application ordered can be – and often is – very wide, potentially encompassing extended family, friends carers and care workers.

It should be kept in mind that the Court retains an inherent power to appoint a safeguarder or *curator ad litem* to the adult, both for applications at first instance, as well as for appeals. The L&B practice note requires the solicitor acting for the applicant for a guardianship order to send a copy of the application and relevant accompanying reports and any answers lodged to a safeguarder or *curator ad litem* within two working days of their appointment [37].

In the first instance, where the Court has fixed a hearing on the application, this must take place not more than 28 days after the relative interlocutor is issued [38]. In cases where the imposition of some measures is sought as a matter of urgency, it seems possible to make averments seeking the shortening of the time prior to a full hearing. However, allowance of a proper time for entering opposition and lodging answers to the application, allied to the availability of Court time may also militate against obtaining an early full hearing.

The Sheriff can decide, where appropriate, that a hearing can take place in any place other than the court building, including a hospital, and also whether the hearing should be held in private [39]. Where an interim guardianship is sought, it may be necessary for the Sheriff to be addressed in chambers.

That said, it recently has been clarified by the Sheriff Appeal Court [40] that that the Sheriff considering a Summary Application under the 2000 Act enjoys a wide discretion over the conduct of proceedings [41], and a Party does not have the absolute right to insist on a Proof [42]. Nevertheless, where there are competing applications for guardianship which involved disputed facts material to the sheriff's decision, it is appropriate for the court to hear evidence in some form [43]

Finding caution

As a generality, any individual appointed to act as a financial guardian – whether or not in conjunction with a welfare guardianship – requires to find caution or such other form of security which the Sheriff thinks fit [44]. Caution generally is either a sum of money or an insurance bond as surety against any loss caused to the adult's estate in the course of the guardianship [45]. The amount of caution and the period for which it will last is fixed at the time the Sheriff issues an interlocutor authorising or appointing the guardian [46] Any caution obtained requires to be lodged with the public guardian [47].

It should be noted that the Court has a discretion whether to require caution to be found, and it can dispense with caution altogether, albeit this may be a rare occurrence. Caution can also be fixed as a percentage of adult's estate from time to time. In the case of *Cooper, Appellant* [48], SP Young clarified that reliance could not be placed on the professional indemnity insurance held by a solicitors' firm or the solicitors' guarantee fund in substitution for a solicitor obtaining caution in order to act as a guardian.

Following the coming into force of the 2000 Act, an applicant normally obtained an individual insurance bond by way of providing caution. (Initially, annual premiums of 0.75% of the adult's estate were being quoted). However, in 2008, the public guardian negotiated a master policy with established insurers.

As published in 2024, the range of premiums spanned, according to the value of the estate concerned:

£20K (£33), £100K (£121), £500K (£56), Increases £11 per £10K

Alternative forms of security, such as consignation of cash or obtaining a separate insurance bond, if the applicant so elects, may also prove acceptable to the Court.

Period of the guardianship order

The default period of a guardianship order is 3 years. However, "on cause shown", the order can be authorised for "a longer or for an indefinite period" [49]. Considerations relevant to extension of the period of a guardianship order beyond 3 years might include that:-

- The adult's condition may be unlikely to change over their life span

- The adult may have limited life – expectancy as the result of a terminal illness

- Avoiding the expense and paperwork of the renewal process, which calls substantially for the same procedure to be carried as for the initial order [50]

Against that, granting an order for a prolonged or indefinite period connotes that no direct judicial review may occur of the need for the guardianship itself, or whether it should continue or continue in its present form. In *Application in relation to M* [51], Sheriff Baird expressed the view that the art. 12(4) of the CRPD [52], which provides that measures should apply for the shortest time possible and should be subject to regular review by a competent, independent and impartial authority or judicial body, pointed to the default period of three years for a guardianship as being more consistent with the aims of the CRPD, than an indefinite order [53].

Another practical example is *North Ayrshire Council v M* [54], where a dispute between the local authority and the wife of an incapable adult, who was due to be moved into a nursing home for a period of 18 – 24 months, regarding his future care planning had arisen. The appointment of the wife as welfare guardian was restricted to 2 years to ensure that the Court could consider what should be the next move by the adult. The potential to avoid investigation by the public guardian and / or MWCS by adopting this course was also seen as advantageous.

Appointment of interim guardian

As mentioned, circumstances may render it essential that some powers are granted to a prospective guardian in the interests of the affected adult as a matter of urgency. Accordingly, it is possible to seek the award of an interim guardianship embracing some or all of the powers contained in the application itself [55]. Such appointment lasts until a guardian is appointed or the "effective period" has ended. The "effective period" runs for three months from the date of appointment of the interim guardian, or such longer period of up to six months from the appointment that the Sheriff specifies [56].

Where the appointment of an interim guardianship is intended or anticipated, the application may require to specify what powers are being sought at that stage, so as to distinguish these from the full powers being applied for, as also to justify the granting of an interim guardianship prior to a hearing. [57]. If the appointment of an interim guardian is not sought in the application itself, such appointment still can be sought by motion [58].

It is submitted that interim guardianship also can be granted where the Court is satisfied that "no other means available under the Act would be sufficient to meet the requirements to protect the property, financial affairs and welfare of the adult" [59]. Satisfaction of such a test necessitates examining whether guardianship is required at all, or whether a lesser measure, such as obtaining an intervention order [60] or authority to intromit with funds [61] is more appropriate to the adult's needs.

During the period an interim guardian holds office, they will be subject to reporting requirements to the public guardian, if exercising financial powers or to the CWSO of the local authority for their area, where exercising welfare powers [62].

Interim guardianship cannot be used simply as a means of preserving the status quo. It also seems that reliance on directions as an alternative to seeking guardianship is likely to be disapproved [63].

### Refusal of a guardianship order

A number of means are available to a Court considering a guardianship application, where it is not satisfied that awarding guardianship is the appropriate disposal. For example, it is open to the Court, having considered the various matters outlined previously, to refuse to appoint the applicant to act as guardian. The Court in all instances must consider the principle of no intervention without benefit to the adult, and may refuse an application as being in conflict with this principle [64].

Moreover, in *Arthur v Arthur* [65], the Sheriff affirmed that s.59 of the 2000 Act meant what it said, and that the Sheriff could appoint "any individual" considered suitable as guardian, even if not the original applicant nor a minuter. Thus, the Court ultimately could appoint someone known to the Court to be suitable for the office [66]. In addition, it is possible, for other parties to seek to make a counter – application for appointment by minute even where the minuter sought appointment as sole guardian, in circumstances where the previously appointed guardian was seeking renewal of her sole guardianship [67].

The Court also can dispose of an application for guardianship by making an intervention order, if satisfied this would be sufficient to meet the "no other means" test specified in 2000 Act, s.58 (1) (b). If so, the court can treat the application as having been made for an intervention order see below and make such order as it deems appropriate [68].

Finally, the Court may also refuse to grant or make any kind of order sought in response to an application. Clearly, a refusal this may necessitate the taking of other actions in order to protect a vulnerable adult including measures available under, for example, the Adult Support and Protection (Scotland) Act 2007.

### Granting of a guardianship order

Where evidence is heard in the course of a Summary Application for a guardianship order, a written judgment incorporating findings in fact and law and setting out the reasons for the decision is necessary [69]. Where the Court grants a guardianship order, the sheriff clerk will notify the public guardian of the terms of the relevant interlocutor. In turn, the public guardian will enter the appointment in the public register, and issue the guardian with a certificate of appointment, as well as notifying the adult, the local authority in which the adult resides, and MWCS where the incapacity results from mental disorder, and welfare powers are granted [70]. Where authority is granted over heritable property, the public guardian also will advise the keeper of the registers [71].

### Granting of guardianship in relation to young adults

It would clearly be unsatisfactory for a gap to be created between a young person with incapacity leaving the regime created by the Children (Scotland) Act 1995 and / or the children's hearings system and the 2000 Act. Accordingly, an application for a guardianship order can be made during the three months preceding a child's 16th birthday, which can be granted by the Court on the basis that it does not take effect until that child becomes an adult on reaching that birthday [72].

## NOTES (CHAPTER 9)

1. 2000 Act, s 58(1) (b).

2. The website of the public guardian records that in 2022-23, 3,235 guardianship orders were registered. Of these, 1,809 contained both financial and welfare powers; 150 financial powers only; and 1,276 welfare powers only.

3. 2000 Act, s.57 (3) (b). The form of the report is specified in the Adults with Incapacity (Reports in relation to Guardianship and Intervention Orders) (Scotland) Regulations 2000, Schd 1. ("The reporting regulations"). At the time of writing, the Scottish Government is consulting on whether a single report from a medical practitioner, GP or clinical psychologist should be sufficient to found an application for a Guardianship Order or Intervention Order.

4. 2000 Act, s.57 (3) (a).

5. 2000 Act, s. 57 (3A) & (3B). This resolves any uncertainty arising from the decision in *Stork Petitioner* 2004 SCLR 513 See also reference to *H Applicant* in Chapter 4 above.

6. 2000 Act, s.57 (3) (a). The term is defined in 2000 Act, s.57 (6B) See Chapter 4 above. Where, for example, the adult experiences an inability to communicate only, the requirement for a report to come from a "relevant medical practitioner" can be disregarded.

7. 2000 Act, s,57 (3) (b) & (c). The form is specified in Schd.8 of the reporting regulations. An extensive range of persons to be consulted in connection with the report is specified in the form.

8. See Chapter 3 above.

9. See Chapter 4 above.

10. See the reporting regulations, Schd.2.

11. 2000 Act, s.57 (3)(b)(i).

12. 2000 Act, s.57 (3)(b)(ii).

13. 2017 SLT 1181.

14. The MHO Report can be written by the CWSO where the welfare of an adult is in jeopardy only by reason of an inability to communicate (2000 Act, s.57 (3) (b)).

15. See Chapter 4 above.

16. See Chapter 16 below.

17. L&B practice note, paras.3(g). *LM v Renfrewshire Council 2024 SLT (SAC) 55* has offered some clarity regarding the correct procedure to be adopted where Guardianship proceedings have been commenced by Summary Application. The Sheriff Appeal Court held that where an application was made in such proceedings for appointment of a nearest relative, the combined effect of s.2 of the 2000 Act and r.2.30 of the SAR gave the Sheriff very wide powers to consider "any motion relating to a summary application" and thus did not require a separate Summary Application to be lodged (At para.15). See reference to *J Solicitor, Applicant* in Chapter 8. above. Detailed provisions regarding making Appeals also form part of the Practice Note.

18. SAR, r..3.16.5.

19. SAR, r.3.16.5(3). See 2003 Act, s.22(4) for the definition of an "approved medical practitioner".

20. It is submitted that the issue of dispensing with intimation to the Adult will warrant particular scrutiny in the light of the decision

of the English Court of Protection in *Aberdeenshire Council v SF (No.2) [2024] EWCOP 10* (See Chapter 24 below).

21. 2000 Act, s.57 (5).

22. SAR, r.3.16.11.

23. See FN 63 below.

24. See L&B practice note, para.3 (e).

25. See L&B practice note, para.3 (r).

26. See Chapter 18 below.

27. See 2000 Act, s.58 (4).

28. L&B practice note, para.3 (o).

29. L&B practice note, para.3 (r).

30. 2017 SLT 1181.

31. At para.19. See SAR r.3.16.8. See also L & B Practice Note para (1) (v), which states that, if a counter-proposal for appointment of a different guardian is sought to be advanced in answers, craves complying with this Practice Note should be included in such answers. The court will then order intimation of the answers including such craves to all interested persons in the same way as has applied to a minute containing such craves.

32. See SAR r.3.16.5.

33. See Chapter 18 below.

34. See Chapter 11 below.

35. See Chapter 21 below.

36. SAR, r.3.16.2.

37. See FN 10 above.

38. L&B Practice Note, paras.3 (aa) and 4 (l).

39. SAR rr.2.31 and 3.16.2.

40. SAR r.3.16.3

41. *Boyle v Denton 2024 SLT SAC 113.*

42. At paras. 31-32.

43. At para.37.

44. At paras.50-55. See also *Miller v Miller 2023 SLT (SAC) 33.*

45. 2000 Act, s.58 (6).

46. See Chapter 17 below in relation to s.82 of the 2000 Act and relief from liability.

47. SAR, r.3.16.10 (1) & (1A). See also Sheriff Courts (Scotland) Act 1907, Part 27.

48. SAR, r.3.16.10 (3).

49. 2009 SLT (Sh.Ct.) 101.

50. 2000 Act, s.58 (4).

51. See L&B practice note, para.3 (r) regarding insertion of an appropriate crave, and Chapter 24 below.

52. 2012 SLT (Sh.Ct.) 25, concerning a guardianship order made in criminal proceedings. See also the method of calculating the

appropriate period considered in *D v Falkirk Council 2023 GWD 10-110* at paras.131–2.

53. At paras.72–3.

54. See Chapter 24 below.

55. 2004 SCLR 956.

56. 2000 Act, s.57 (5).

57. 2000 Act, s.57 (5) & (6).

58. See also L&B practice note, para.3(m).

59. SAR, r.3.16.11. In *D v Falkirk Council*, the Court refused to grant part of a Guardianship Order on the basis that an Intervention Order could be sought if the power sought required to be authorised subsequently (At para.123).

60. 2000 Act, s.58 (b).

61. See Chapter 14 below.

62. See Chapter 16 below.

63. See Chapter 17 below.

64. *G v West Lothian Council* 2015 GWD 40 – 730.

65. See Chapter 2 above.

66. 2005 SCLR 350. This decision established that it was competent to enter the guardianship process by minute. See also reference to *Aberdeenshire Council v JM* and SARr.3.16.8 above.

67. At 353 C-D.

68. *M v M* 2014 SLT (Sh.Ct.) 37.

69. 2000 Act, s.58 (3). See also Chapter 14 below. The Sheriff is also obliged to "have regard" to any intervention order or guardianship order previously made in relation to the adult (2000 Act, ss.58 (2)) & (7)).

70. *Boyle v Denton 2024 SLT (SAC) 113* at para.54. See Sheriff Courts Act 1907, s.50).

71. 2000 Act, s.61.

72. 2000 Act, s.79A. Arrangements relating to children under the age of 18 will require to operate conform to the United Nations Convention on the Rights of the Child (Incorporation) (Scotland) Act 2024 where a "child" is defined as a person under that age (2024 Act, Schedule, Art.1).

# CHAPTER TEN

# ONCE A GUARDIANSHIP ORDER IS OBTAINED

What is the effect of a guardianship order?

The 2000 Act provides that when a guardianship order is granted:-

> "The adult shall have *no capacity* to enter into any transaction in relation to any matter which is within the scope of the authority conferred upon the guardian…" [1]

Accordingly, insofar as any matter comprised in a guardianship order is concerned, legal agency for that is transferred from the adult to the guardian in its entirety. While such a complete divestiture has the benefit of creating certainty, it represents a stronger provision of stripping capacity that operates in other regimes. For example, for England and Wales, the Mental Capacity Act 2005, states that:-

> "A person is not to be treated as unable to make a decision unless all practicable steps to help him to do so have been taken without success". [2]

It is submitted that consideration must be given in appropriate cases to ensuring that the adult is aware, and is encouraged to use, such capacity as is left after the guardianship order is made. In this regard, it is important to note that the 2000 Act requires:-

> "Any guardian… exercising functions under this Act or under any order of the sheriff in relation to an adult shall, in so far as it is reasonable and practicable to do so, encourage the adult to exercise whatever skills he has concerning his property, financial affairs or

> personal welfare, as the case may be, and to develop new such skills." [3].

Moreover, Art 12.2 of the CRPD declares that:

> "persons with disabilities enjoy legal capacity on an equal basis with others in all aspects of life" [4].

As such, any pressure to seek maximum divestiture of the adult's capacity requires to be balanced against such considerations. In consequence of being issued with a certificate of registration, a financial guardian can take possession of any estate of the adult, and also direct that payments go from the adult to the financial guardian.

A financial guardian is entitled to act – insofar as not expressly prohibited by the Sheriff and subject to any conditions and restrictions contained in the guardianship order – to act as the adult's legal representative in relation to any matter within the scope of the powers created by the guardianship order [5]. In broad terms, a financial guardian is entitled to use the capital and income of an adult's estate in order to purchase "assets, services or accommodation", so as to enhance the adult's quality of life [6].

Where a guardianship order vests in the guardian any right of the adult to heritable property, the Sheriff must specify each property in sufficient terms to allow its registration in the land register or Register of Sasines [7], which will allow the financial guardian to apply for the updating of the title sheet of Register of Sasines applying to any such properties [8].

A financial guardian can authorise the adult to carry out "such transactions or category of transactions" as the guardian may specify [9]. This can be operated consistently with the five principles, and one suggestion in the *Code of practice for persons authorised under intervention orders and guardians* [10] is delegating the spending of small amounts of pocket money, or the exercise of an annual clothing allowance to the adult [11].

Provision is made for circumstances where the adult fails to comply with a direction of a welfare guardian which "the adult might reasonably be expected to comply with" [12].

The relevant Regulations are the Adults with Incapacity (Non – Compliance with Decisions of Welfare Guardians) (Scotland) Regulations 2002. ("the non-compliance regulations"). These provide that an application can be made to the Sheriff Court setting out:

- Details of the decision not being complied with
- The person failing to comply with the direction
- What had been done to achieve compliance
- The whereabouts of the adult, if different from the address stated in the application [13]

Ultimately, failure to comply with such directions may result in an order for the adult to comply with the decision of a guardian [14], or where the matter relates to the place of residence of the adult, a warrant being granted for a constable to enter premises and to apprehend and remove the adult "to such place as the guardian may direct" [15].

As noted previously, in practice, it may be that that a choice requires to be made between resort to the 2002 Regulations and measures available under the Adult Support and Protection (Scotland) Act 2007, such as a removal order [16], where the former cannot achieve the desired level of protection with sufficient speed.

## NOTES (CHAPTER 10)

1. 2000 Act, s.67 (1) (Emphasis added). It was established in *G's Guardians v Greater Glasgow Health Board 2021 GWD 40-533* that the removal of an adult's capacity to enter "transactions" which fall within a Guardianship Order includes their ability to consent to medical treatments (At para.8). S.67 (1) – (3) of the 2000 Act applies with modifications in relation to an Intervention Order (2000 Act, s.53 (14)). In *G's* Guardians, the Sheriff Appeal Court explicitly stated that the powers invested in a Guardian under s.70 of the 2000 Act [(or holder of an Intervention Order)] should not trespass on decisions which as a matter of medical ethics and as a matter of law are clinical judgements (At para.12. See also Chapter 23 below).

2. Mental Capacity Act 2005, s.1(3).

3. 2000 Act, s.1 (5).

4. See Chapter 24 below.

5. 2000 Act, s.64 (3).

6. 2000 Act, s.64 (5). See, however consideration of the formulation of the terms of a management plan in Chapter 17 below.

7. 2000 Act, s.61 (1) & (2).

8. 2000 Act, s.61 (5) & (6).

9. 2000 Act, s.64 (1)(e).

10. *Code of practice for persons authorised under intervention orders and guardians* (Scottish Government) (2018)

11. *Code of practice for persons authorised under intervention orders and guardians*, para.5.60

12. 2000 Act, s.70 (1) & (2).

13. Non – compliance regulations, Schedule.

14. 2000 Act, s.70 (1) (a).

15. 2000 Act, s70 (1) (b). See also 2000 Act, s.70 (3) – (4A). An example of an application made under s.70 of the 2000 Act can be found in *City of Edinburgh Council v D* 2011 SLT (Sh.Ct.) 15. See *K v Argyll and Bute Council 2023 SLT 293*, where the s.70 procedure was described as an additional safeguard against misuse of a guardian's powers under s.64 of the 2000 Act (At para.33). See also Chapter 20 below.

16. 2007 Act, s.14. See Chapter 22 below.

# CHAPTER ELEVEN

# MANAGING A GUARDIANSHIP ORDER

The specific authority passed to a guardian will be defined by the terms of the guardianship order itself. It is important to recall that the wording will circumscribe the extent of the guardian's authority [1]. In general, the matters most likely to occur are:-

- Dealing with the property, financial affairs and personal welfare of the adult

- Dealing with aspects of the personal welfare of the adult

- Exercising power to pursue or defend certain legal actions (divorce and separation) [2]

- Management of the adult's property and financial affairs [3].

- Providing authority for a welfare guardian to consent to the carrying out of medical treatment on the adult, as can be authorised under s.47 of the 2000 Act [4]

How a financial guardian manages an adult's affairs

The process of managing the estate of an adult who is subject to financial guardianship is conducted subject to the supervision of the public guardian [5]. As operated by the public guardian, the process contains two elements. The first is compilation of an inventory of the adult's estate, allowing for the ingathering of estate as authorised by the guardianship order, followed by lodging of the inventory itself with the public guardian, along with a draft management plan. The second stage is the preparation of a management plan for dealing with the estate for approval by the public guardian.

Thus, a financial guardian initially is restricted to ingathering and taking assets of the adult under control and making necessary payments on behalf of the adult until the public guardian has approved a management plan [6].

The form of an inventory is provided on the public guardian's website and may include:

- buildings, land and other heritable property;
- vehicles;
- cash, bank accounts, building society accounts, ISAs, money held in the post office or a credit union, etc.;
- moveable property such as furniture, ornaments, jewellery, household equipment, electronics;
- stocks and shares;
- business assets and interests;
- debts owed to the adult:
- life assurance policies where there is a cash return expected;
- compensation payable to the adult now or at some stage in the future; under a structured settlement;
- the adult's income, e.g. from benefits, annuities or rents

Part of the process may include obtaining a proof of ownership of major items [7].

The public guardian is entitled to dispense with the requirement to produce an inventory and can require the financial guardian to take such other action in lieu as thought appropriate [8]. The form of a management plan is also available on the public guardian's website.

The five principles will apply equally to the conduct of management of the adult's estate. The *Code of practice for anyone authorised under any intervention or guardianship order* ("*the code of practice*") advises that: -

> "Benefit to the adult must be seen as relating to his or her likely means both now and in the future. It would not be sensible to use funds to procure large benefits now, at the risk of leaving the adult inadequately provided for at a later stage in life. In determining this, full account must of course be taken of the adult's realistic expectations of other income by way of pensions, state benefits, etc" [9].

Implicit in such advice is an activist approach on the guardian's part, extending considerably beyond that of preservation of the estate as was the remit of a *curator bonis*. This will entail consideration of the likely future of the adult in the medium term at least, and will mandate formulation of specific and clear proposals for future management. Part of this process may also entail a financial guardian seeking additional powers from the Sheriff Court if existing provisions are inadequate in some way.

Overall, the aim will be to satisfy the public guardian that a proactive approach will be taken to this responsibility. This is consistent with the statutory empowerment of a finanacial guardian to:-

> "use the capital and income of the adult's estate for the purpose of purchasing assets, accommodation or services so enhance the adult's quality of life [10].

This will involve an assessment of whether the adult's finances are in a "satisfactory shape", combined with looking to the future, including:-

- the renewal of any lease;
- the repayment of any outstanding loan;
- the reinvestment of any funds that reach maturity, such as a life assurance policy;
- the future support of any persons for whom the adult had accepted some responsibility;
- any possible move to residential care [11].

This further implies formulating positive proposals for the future management of the adult's estate. Again, it may be that completion of this process denotes the need for variation of powers under the guardianship order or making an application for an intervention order.

The normal elements expected of a management plan satisfactory to the public guardian include:-

- assessment of the adult's likely ordinary living expenses
- specification of the intended use of any heritable property belonging to the adult; [12]
- proposals for the use and disposal of assets
- tax planning proposals

It is also expected that contact with the adult will be maintained.

The public guardian's website provides worked examples of a management plan and also extensive guidance on the expected components. The fee for approval by the public guardian of the inventory and management plan is calculated on an *ad valorem* basis [13].

Effect of approval of a management plan

Once the management plan has been approved, a financial guardian will be expected generally to exercise the powers granted in accordance with its terms, the five principles, and also the *Code of practice*. [14].

A financial guardian is likely to wish to make arrangements for the deposit and withdrawal of cash or internet accounts, as well as the management of investments and making new investments. A financial guardian is required to keep any investment under review, and requires to operate in accordance with the further principles that: -

> "(a) that the investment must be prudent;
>
> (b) that there must be diversification of investments; and
>
> (c) that the investment must be suitable for the adult's estate." [15].

A financial guardian requires to obtain and consider professional advice (described as "proper advice") where the value of the adult's estate exceeds £50,000 [16].

An important part of a management plan is specifying what arrangements can be made for gifts the adult may have wished to make when capable. Such gifts normally require the authorisation of the public guardian. The public guardian website has a form by which a financial guardian can seek authority to make gifts on either a general or specific basis [17]

A financial guardian can delegate or appoint someone to carry out their functions, but responsibility for conduct of the adult's estate will remain with the financial guardian for the conduct of such matters in the first instance [18].

Some exceptions apply to the generality of a financial guardian's authority while a guardianship order is in force, where the consent of the public guardian is required. One common instance concerns the purchase and sale of "accommodation" for the adult where the public guardian's approval is required at two stages (Application for consent in principle to the transaction and consent to the proposed selling price) [19].

Where objections are raised by persons notified of the application in principle of the transaction, the public guardian must remit the matter to the Sheriff for determination. The same process operates where the public guardian determines to refuse an application in principle [20]. The public guardian is entitled to grant the application in principle having considered any objections, and any person who objects to the decision of the public guardian at this stage also may have the matter remitted to the Sheriff for determination [21].

The conduct of a welfare guardianship

Where welfare powers are granted in a guardianship order, it is likely that these will be fairly broadly drawn. Possible examples of exercise of such powers, which require to occur in compliance with the five principles and the *Code of practice* could include: -

- Moving an adult into supported accommodation
- Supporting an adult who has suffered a form of brain damage
- Protecting an adult with learning disability during a proposal to move the adult into supported accommodation [22].

Other examples of applying the five principles given in the *Code of practice* include:-

- Benefit: Where an adult apparently is losing weight while in a care home. What might a change in their regime achieve?

Possibilities include discussion of the adult's diet, seeking review of the adult's care plan or seeking a medical assessment

- Least restrictive option: Securing more support at home in preference to admission of the adult to a care home

- Adult's views: It is not uncommon for an adult to express a wish of "Not wanting to be a burden on the family". What alternatives or reassurance can be provided to the adult? [23].

It should be stressed that these are merely examples of application of the five principles to one common situation. In principle, a similar kind of evaluation is desiderated for any decision of significance taken by a welfare guardian.

A further aspect of the discharge of the obligations of both a financial and welfare guardian are duties specified in the *Code of practice.* In essence these are the three duties considered in Chapter 7 in an appropriately modified form. These are a duty of care; a fiduciary duty; and a duty of confidentiality, which are intended to be applied in a similar fashion as by attorneys [24].

A further duty is that of notifying the public guardian of a change of the adult's address within seven days of this occurring. The 2000 Act does not expressly require notification of the death of the adult in a similar manner [25].

What else must a guardian do?

> "A guardian shall keep records of the exercise of their power" [26].

It will be noted that this requirement is couched, as with attorneys, in the most broad terms [27]. In this instance, a guardian is both an appointee of a Court and subject to the supervision of the public guardian and / or the local authority. What level of recording might be appropriate to satisfy such supervision?

In the case of a welfare guardian, the *Code of practice* suggests that the required records might amount to little more than a background file (contacts etc.), but should also record the use of powers as they concern "major actions or decisions" [28]. Other suggested matters include:-

- Recording whether the adult has strong views regarding living in residential care;

- Retaining copies of relevant correspondence and notes of telephone calls particularly with other people having an interest in the adult's welfare;

- Retaining copies of invoices or receipts in order to obtain sanction for reimbursement from the public guardian [29].

The position of a financial guardian is more closely prescribed. A financial guardian is required to submit accounts to the public guardian. In general, this initially will entail providing accounts covering the first 18 months of management of the adult's estate from the date of appointment of the financial guardian, and thereafter annually [30]. The periods specified – which can be changed by the public guardian – are termed "accounting periods", and accounts must be submitted to the public guardian within one month of the end of each accounting period [31].

Accounts must be submitted in a form prescribed by the public guardian who can give directions as to the frequency of accounting periods, and can also dispense with the need for submission of accounts by the financial guardian and require submission of anything considered appropriate in lieu of submitting accounts [32]. Where a financial guardian manages an adult's estate which includes a business or an interest in a business, the accuracy of the business accounts must be separately submitted for audit by the public guardian [33].

Above this, any accounts which are submitted to the public guardian must be audited to determine whether the accounts offer:-

> "a true and fair management of the guardian's management of the adult's estate." [34].

If so, the public guardian can approve the accounts, and also can do so, where the public guardian is satisfied that the financial guardian has acted "reasonably and in good faith". If satisfied on either basis, the public guardian can approve the accounts and fix the remuneration of the financial guardian [35].

Where the public guardian considers that the accounts submitted do not reach the specified standards, a report can be prepared as to the extent of any shortcoming and adjusting the accounts accordingly. Such a report is sent, in the first instance, to the financial guardian who has 28 days from dispatch of the report to object to the public guardian's findings. If such objection is not resolved between the public guardian and the financial guardian, the financial guardian can apply for the matter to be determined by the Sheriff, whose decision on the matter is "final" [36].

Where the accounts are finally approved by the public guardian, the financial guardian will be liable for any deficiency revealed by the accounts, which can include interest on the amount of the deficiency [37]. In such circumstances, it is likely that resort would be made initially to any bond of caution lodged during the application for financial guardianship powers [38].

This process may generate proposals for changing the management plan, which both the financial guardian and public guardian are required to keep under review and submit proposals for variation at any time. In the case of any amendments proposed by the public guardian, the financial guardian is entitled to make objections to these before the public guardian makes any such variation [39].

### Professional guardianship scheme

A system for the submission of accounts by professional firms or LLPs was introduced by the public guardian in 2017. The aim is to facilitate the self certification of accounts by financial guardians, who have satisfied the public guardian by their previous satisfactory supply of "clean accounts" which are examined subsequently on a reducing basis [40].

How should a guardian take decisions?

Notwithstanding the detailed provisions of statute and guidance, and at the risk of repetition, the fundamental guiding consideration in the conduct of a guardianship is one of applying the five principles in the conduct of an adult's estate and in supporting their welfare. Part of achieving this aim will be the undertaking of consultation with appropriate people (family, friends, professionals) – and where appropriate, the statutory bodies – at appropriate times.

Nevertheless, the overriding message to guardians who have adopted such an approach is not to back down where confident in their judgement. To back down on an issue may have the effect of letting down an adult and leaving them without someone to make decisions on their behalf, especially in the field of their welfare [41].

## NOTES (CHAPTER 11)

1. See *H's Guardian v H* 2013 SLT (Sh.Ct.) 31 and *G v West Lothian Council* 2014 GWD 40-730. See Chapter 10 FN 1 above.

2. In *H's Guardian v H*, the power to pursue an action of divorce (See 2000 Act, s.64 (1) (c)) was not included in an application to renew a financial guardianship. The means found for remedying such an omission is by lodging a minute seeking extra powers (See *MM's Guardian* 2012 GWD 39-770).

3. Other effects of a guardianship order on an adult could, for example, include empowering the guardian to make a nationality declaration.

4. See Chapter 23 below. A welfare guardian cannot place an adult in a hospital for "the treatment of mental disorder against [their] will" (2000 Act, s.64 (2) (a)). See also *G's Guardians v Greater Glasgow Health Board 2021 GWD 40-533.*

5. See Chapter 17 below.

6. 2000 Act, Sched.1, para.1(4)). Detailed advice on the content of an inventory is provided in the guidance notes and inventory form provided on the public guardian's website. It is likely that some latitude will be granted where, a financial guardian requires to keep a business running or there is an urgent need to sell an asset.

7. The public guardian's website provides worked examples of proof obtained from banks, pension providers etc.

8. 2000 Act, Sched. 2, para.3.

9. *Code of practice for persons authorised under intervention orders and guardians* ("*the Code of practice*") (Scottish Government) (2018), para.5.20.

10. *Code of practice,* para.5.20.

11. *Code of practice,* para.5.32. Similar consideration may also be appropriate in relation to community care services (para.5.29).

12. Public guardian website, guidance notes and management plan. For the provisions relating to the sale and purchase of a dwellinghouse or provision of accommodation for the adult, see Chapter 19 below.

13. See Chapter 18 below.

14. Chapter 5 of the *Code of practice* is particularly relevant in this respect. Specifically, the public guardian has stated that its consent is not required where an adult will "benefit directly" and the five principles have been taken into consideration (Public guardian website).

15. 2000 Act, Sched.2, para.5 (3). The public guardian can direct a financial guardian to realise any investment (Sched. 2, para.5 (4).

16. 2000 Act, Sched 2, para.5 (1) – (3). The figure of £50,000 is specified on the public guardian website in the guidance relating to management plans.

17. Normally, the making of gifts of less that £100 will not require authorisation by the public guardian (Public guardian website, guidance notes and management plan).

18. 2000 Act, s.64 (6).

19. 2000 Act, Sched. 2, para.6 (1).

20. 2000 Act, Sched.2, paras. 6 (2) – (4).

21. 2000 Act, Sched.2, para.6 (5) & (6). The decision of the Sheriff on any matter remitted under Sched.3, Para.6 is stated to be "final" (See also Chapter 17 below).

22. *Code of practice*, para.6.9.

23. *Code of practice*, paras.6.22 and 6.45.

24. *Code of practice*, paras.5.1 & 6.1. For welfare guardians, the duty of confidentiality is expressed as embracing a right of access to confidential information about the adult; use and proper disclosure of such information, as well as the fiduciary duty.

25. 2000 Act, s.64 (4). The death of an adult causes a guardianship order to "cease to have effect" (2000 Act, s.77 (1)), but does not create an express duty to notify the public guardian (See Chapter 19 below). Nevertheless, it will be good practice to provide such notification, as various formalities will require to be completed with the public guardian (See Chapter 17 below).

26. 2000 Act, s.65.

27. See Chapter 7 above.

28. *Code of practice*, para.6.43.

29. *Code of practice*, para.6.45.

30. 2000 Act, Sched.2, para.7.

31. 2000 Act, Sched.2, para.7 (1) & (3).

32. 2000 Act, Sched.2, para.7 (4) & (5).

33. 2000 Act, Sched 2, para.7 (6) & (7).

34. 2000 Act, Sched. 2, para.8 (1) (a).

35. 2000 Act, Sched.2, para.8 (1) & (2). See also Chapter 17 below.

36. 2000 Act, Sched 2, para.8 (3) – (5). See also Chapter 17 below.

37. 2000 Act ,Sched 2, para.8 (7).

38. See Chapter 9 above and Chapter 17 below regarding where personal liability may attach to a financial guardian.

39. 2000 Act, Sched.2, para.1 (6) – (9).

40. Fuller details of the professional guardianship scheme (Scheme for professionals), including detailed terms and conditions of membership are available on the public guardian's website. The scheme is open to professional firms who have five or more guardianship cases.

41. *Code of practice*, para.5.45.

# CHAPTER TWELVE

# HOW GUARDIANSHIP CAN WORK

There are several manners in which appointment of a guardian can be achieved under the 2000 Act

Joint guardianship

It is possible to apply for, and for the Sheriff Court to appoint

> "two or more individuals"

or

> "an individual…for appointment as an additional guardian to an adult jointly with one or more existing guardians" [1]

The underlying intention behind joint guardianship is to allow family members to discharge the role jointly, as is made clear by the further provision that:-

> "Joint guardians shall not be appointed to an adult unless….the individuals so appointed are parents, siblings or children of the adult"

unless:

> "the Sheriff is satisfied that, in the circumstances, it is appropriate to appoint someone not [so] related to the adult…" [2].

In the first instance, the same criteria apply to the appointment of individuals seeking to be appointed as joint guardians as applies to a sole applicant [3]. Where appointment as an additional joint guardian is sought, the Sheriff is also directed to "have regard to" the matters set out in the 2000 Act, s.59 (3) – (5) [4].

In such instances, it is important to employ the correct procedural step. In the case of *Cooke v Telford* [5], a relative had lodged answers – as opposed to a minute – to an application for appointment as financial guardian to her aunt, who was the sister of the respondent.

The respondent sought appointment as sole or joint guardian of the adult. The failure to lodge a separate minute [6] was held to have resulted in the respondent's application being found to be incompetent. Further, the respondent could not use the process to have herself appointed as joint guardian in an opposed application [7].

However, there is a distinction made between an application to appoint joint guardians, and an individual seeking to intervene via a counter-proposal [8]. The L&B practice note requires averments to be made establishing the suitability of a proposal to appoint joint guardians against the general tests [9]. The Sheriff may refuse to appoint a joint guardian where an evidently acrimonious relationship exists between any of the prospective office – holders [10].

Once appointed, joint guardians are entitled to exercise their functions individually, and each guardian shall be liable for any loss or injury caused to the adult arising out of—

> (a) his own acts or omissions; or
>
> (b) his failure to take reasonable steps to ensure that a joint guardian does not breach any duty of care or fiduciary duty owed to the adult

and where more than one such guardian is liable; they shall be liable jointly and severally" [11].

The 2000 Act aims to avoid disputes regarding the administration of the adult's estate by requiring that:-

> "A joint guardian shall, before exercising any functions conferred on him, consult the other joint guardians, unless—
>
> (a) consultation would be impracticable in the circumstances; or
>
> (b) the joint guardians agree that consultation is not necessary." [12].

In the event of a dispute, one or both of the joint guardians are entitled to apply to the Sheriff for directions in order to resolve the issue [13].

Joint guardians equally are required to demonstrate adherence to, and application of, the five principles, and have a means of keeping records [14].

Substitute guardian

It is possible for the Sheriff Court, in granting a guardianship order to appoint someone to:-

> "act as guardian in the event of the guardian so appointed ["original guardian"] becoming unable to act" [15]

Appointment of a substitute guardian arises "on the death or incapacity of the original guardian". When this arises, the substitute guardian is required to notify the public guardian "without undue delay" of this circumstance – including documentary evidence confirming the death – and whether the substitute guardian is willing to act. Where the substitute guardian has so assented, the public guardian will make the necessary alterations to the public register [16].

Somewhat surprisingly, the 2000 Act does not specify what form of "incapacity" triggers the appointment of a substitute guardian. There are a number of means by which a guardian can be removed from office, but no direct reference is made to a ground of "incapacity" [17]. It is also unclear what kind of physical ailment or disability also achieves the standard of "incapacity" and how that is to be properly vouched. If triggered, a substitute guardian will hold office for the same period as applied to the original guardian and on the same basis, unless specified otherwise in the order making the initial appointment [18].

There is an evident risk that a nominated substitute guardian will not confirm their willingness to take up the position, or be able to find caution for the exercise of any financial powers. The 2000 Act does not make clear what process exists to avoid an adult being pitched into a legal vacuum.

The Sheriff is entitled to appoint an "office holder" as substitute guardian, and thus one possibility might be to appoint the CSWO for the area in which the adult lives as substitute guardian [19]. The L & B practice note requires averments to be made in the summary application that the substitute guardian appointment should take effect on the "death, incapacity or resignation" of the original guardian, which it can be assumed will form part of the interlocutor appointing the substitute guardian. Accordingly, a considerable amount of information regarding a prospective substitute guardian requires to be provided, which may enable the Sheriff to take a view whether the substitute guardian will confirm willingness to take the appointment where required [20].

In the absence of such an appointment, it is open for a "person with an interest in the property, financial affairs or personal welfare" of the adult to apply for the office, or else will local authority will require to step in [21].

## NOTES (CHAPTER 12)

1. 2000 Act, s.62 (1). See *M v M* 2014 SLT (Sh.Ct) 37 where the distinction between the process of applying to be a joint guardian and appointment of an additional guardian (see below) was considered.

2. 2000 Act, s.62 (2). One possible configuration of responsibilities in order to avoid intra – family disputes is appointment of a close relative of the adult or a married couple who act as long – term carers of the adult.

3. 2000 Act, s.62 (3) & (4). See Chapter 9 above.

4. 2000 Act, s.62 (3).

5. 2005 SCLR 367.

6. See reference to *Arthur v Arthur* 2005 SCLR 350 in Chapter 9 above.

7. c.f. *M v M 2015* SLT (Sh.Ct) 37, where Sheriff Morrison rejected an interpretation that an application to be appointed as an additional guardian required to be made jointly (at para.16). See also *LM v Renfrewshire Council* 2024 SLT (SAC) 55.

8. See *JM v Aberdeenshire Council* in Chapter 9 above.

9. L&B practice note, para.3 (o).

10. *M, Applicant,* 2009 GWD 24 – 394.

11. 2000 Act, s.62 (6). A third party acting in good faith is entitled to rely on the authority to act of any one or more joint guardians (2000 Act, s.62 (9)). See Chapter 7 above in relation to the stated duties. See also Chapter 17 below.

12. 2000 Act, s.62 (7).

13. 2000 Act, s.62 (8). See also 2000 Act, s.3 and *Boyle v Denton 2024 SLT (SAC) 113* (at paras. 43-45).

14. See Chapter 11 above.

15. 2000 Act, s.63 (1). Any individual or office holder who could competently have been appointed under the 2000 Act, s.59 can assume the office of "substitute guardian" (s.63 (1) & (6)). (See above).

16. 2000 Act, s.63 (7) – (9).

17. See Chapter 13 below.

18. 2000 Act, s.63 (3), (6) & (10).

19. 2000 Act, s.63 (1).

20. See L&B practice note, para.3 (c), (o) – (p).

21. See 2000 Act, s.57 (2) and Chapter 9 above. Different considerations apply where a guardian seeks to resign their office (See Chapter 13 below).

# CHAPTER THIRTEEN

# OTHER ASPECTS OF GUARDIANSHIP ORDERS

Renewal of powers

As mentioned previously, a guardianship order generally will be granted for a period of 3 years, but can continue for a shorter or longer period, including indefinitely [1]. Renewal generally follows the same procedure as the original application [2], including the obtaining of contemporaneous medical reports. Two medical reports will be required where the adult's incapacity is due to "mental disorder" [3], and MHO report, in addition to a report from the public guardian, where a renewal of financial powers is sought. The report will provide the public guardian's opinion as to:-

(i) the applicant's conduct as the adult's guardian; and

(ii) the suitability of the applicant to continue to be the adult's guardian" [4].

Where the Sheriff grants an application for renewal of a guardianship order, the Sheriff can continue the order for five years or such other period (including an indefinite period) on cause shown, as may be determined [5]. Where the Sheriff determines to refuse the application, the Court must notify the public guardian, who will amend the public register, as also the adult and the local authority where the adult resides. In cases where welfare powers have been granted previously in respect of an adult who has a disability as the result of a "mental disorder", the Court must also advise the MWCS [6].

Essentially, the considerations supporting the original grant of guardianship will require to be satisfied, but equally, the requirements of the five principles will inform a decision to renew powers, and will require justification against their terms [7].

## Variation of a guardianship order

At any time when a guardianship order is in effect, the Sheriff "may vary the powers conferred by the guardianship order" on the application of any person (including the adult himself) claiming an interest in the property, financial affairs or personal welfare of the adult [8].

Where the variation sought relates to financial powers, the court can require the guardian to find caution or some other form of security thought fit [9]. Any variation allowed will be notified by the Court to the public guardian who will amend the public register; and also notify the adult, the local authority where the adult resides. Again, in cases where welfare powers have been granted previously in respect of an adult who has a "disability" as the result of a "mental disorder", the Court will notify the MWCS [10].

Variation of a guardianship order cannot be made so as to add a welfare guardianship to a financial guardianship or vice versa, and such a step requires an application to be made under s.57 in order to effect such a change [11].

## Leaving the office of guardian

There are five specified ways in which a guardian can leave office which are:-

### Death

The death of the adult has the result that the guardianship order applying to them ceases to have effect [12]. In this regard, a guardian who continues to act in good faith until becoming aware of the adult's death is entitled to continue to act under the powers of the guardianship order [13]. A third party is entitled to rely on the authority of a guardian (including a joint guardian) if unaware of the termination or coming to an end of that authority. Similarly, title to any interest in any heritable property acquired in good faith and for value from a guardian with financial powers cannot be challenged only on the grounds of such termination of authority [14].

## Resignation

A joint guardian, or a guardian in respect of whom a substitute guardian has been appointed [15] can resign by giving notice to the public guardian, the local authority where the adult resides, and in cases where welfare powers have granted previously in respect of an adult who has a disability as the result of a "mental disorder", the MWCS [16].

With a view to preventing the creation of a legal vacuum in relation to an adult, a resignation cannot take effect until evidence has been presented to the public guardian that a remaining joint guardian is willing to continue to act, as similarly is any nominated substitute guardian [17]. Further, a guardian cannot resign who either has no joint guardian, has no substitute guardian appointed, or is awaiting the s.75 (2) process being completed, cannot resign until a replacement guardian is appointed [18].

## Replacement

It is possible for the adult or any person claiming an interest in an adult's "property, financial affairs or personal welfare" to apply to the Sheriff for a replacement guardian to be appointed who satisfies the requirements of s.59 (3) – (5) of the 2000 Act. Where an application to appoint a replacement guardian is granted, the Court will notify the public guardian, who will amend the public record, and when satisfied that the replacement guardian has found caution or other security, issue a certificate of appointment [19].

## Removal

Anyone qualified to apply for replacement of a guardian is equally entitled to apply to the Sheriff for removal of a guardian. For such an order to be granted, the Sheriff must be satisfied that:

(a) there is a substitute guardian who is willing to act as guardian; or

(b) where there are joint guardians, that the remaining guardian or guardians are prepared to continue to act [20]. It is unclear what would be the position were remaining joint guardians to disagree about acting subsequent to removal of a joint guardian. In such a situation, resort to other measures available under the 2000 Act may be required.

Where the application is granted, the Court will again notify the public guardian, who will issue a new certificate of appointment to the substitute guardian or remaining joint guardian(s), and also notify the adult, the adult, the local authority where the adult resides, and, in cases where welfare powers have been granted previously in respect of an adult who has a "disability" as the result of a "mental disorder", the MWCS [21].

Recall of powers granted under a guardianship order can be initiated by the public guardian, the local authority in which an adult subject to a guardianship order habitually resides or MWCS, of their own initiative or else on an application to them by the the adult, or else by any person (including the adult himself) claiming an interest in the personal welfare of the adult, where satisfied that:-

(a) the grounds for appointment of a guardian with such powers are no longer fulfilled; or

(b) the interests of the adult in his property and financial affairs can be satisfactorily safeguarded or promoted otherwise than by guardianship [22].

In essence, where such a step is envisaged, the relevant body must intimate their intention to recall the guardianship powers to the adult, their nearest relative, named person and any person they consider has an interest in the recall, and advise them of their right to object to that proposal. Any recall cannot take effect until any objectors to the proposal have had the opportunity to be heard [23].

Where an application for recall made to any of the bodies is proposed to be refused, that intention requires to be intimated to the adult and the applicant. The application cannot be refused until the applicant or adult, should they object to the proposal, have the opportunity to be heard [24].

Provision exists for the remit or making of appeals to the Sheriff, whose determination is stated to be "final". In the case of appeals, the decision being appealed against remains in force until determined by the Sheriff [25]. (The process of recall of a guardianship order, including the prescribed form is specified by the Adults with Incapacity (Recall of Guardians' Powers) (Scotland) Regulations 2002).

## Discharge of a guardian

Termination of the office of financial guardian, whether as the result of the death of the adult or the resignation, replacement, removal, recall of powers, or the expiry of a guardianship order does not terminate the responsibility of the former financial guardian until a discharge is obtained. (This also will be an issue for a guardian's executors where the guardian dies in office).

The granting of a discharge in respect of a former guardian's actings and intromissions with the estate of an adult is a matter for the public guardian in the first instance [26].

Consequently, such a discharge will be granted by the public guardian following an application by the former guardian or the representatives of a guardian who has died, in relation to "the former guardian's acts and intromissions with the estate of the adult" [27].

A process is established for intimation of an application for discharge to the adult, their nearest relative, primary carer, named person and any other person whom the public guardian considers has an interest in the application, and for dealing with objections and decisions to grant or refuse a discharge, and for the "final" determination of issues by the Sheriff [28].

## Criminal procedure

It is competent for a Court dealing with a criminal matter to grant a guardianship order as part of the disposal of a case, or a welfare intervention order as an alternative to making a guardianship order. The arrangements for making a guardianship order under criminal procedure are broadly similar to that under the 2000 Act, and involves consideration by the Court of medical and MHO reports as part of the process.

Such a guardianship order can be granted in favour of an individual or a local authority. The order can be granted for a period of 3 years, or for an indefinite period [29]. In a general sense, the provisions of the 2000 Act apply to a guardianship order so made, and can provide for the appointment of a joint or substitute guardian. The powers granted can only apply to the "personal welfare" of the adult concerned [30].

## NOTES (CHAPTER 13)

1. See Chapter 9 above.

2. 2000 Act, s.60 (1). See Chapter 9 above.

3. 2000 Act, s.60 (3A). See Chapter 2 above.

4. 2000 Act, s.60 (3).

5. 2000 Act, s.58 (4), as substituted for this purpose by s.60 (4).

6. 2000 Act, s.60 (5).

7. The terms of the L&B practice note should be viewed as equally applicable to applications for renewal of a guardianship order (See L&B Practice Note para.3 (d), (f) & (g)).

8. 2000 Act, s.74 (1)). One example of such a step being taken is *Application for Directions, West Lothian Council in respect of Y* 2014 SLT (Sh.Ct.) 93.

9. 2000 Act, s.74 (2).

10. See Chapter 9 above

11. 2000 Act, s.74 (4). See Chapter 8 above.

12. 2000 Act s.77 (1).

13. 2000 Act, s.77 (2). The subsection refers to "or any other event which has the effect of terminating [the] authority", which is relevant to the other means of leaving office considered below.

14. 2000 Act, s.77 (3) & (4).

15. See Chapter 12 above.

16. 2000 Act, s.75 (1).

17. 2000 Act, s.75 (2). See Chapter 12 above. The wording of the subsection appears to assume that only one other joint guardian has been appointed, and it is not clear whether the public guardian requires confirmation from all joint guardians who would remain were a resignation to take effect.

18. 2000 Act, s.75 (5). See also 2000 Act, s.71 and Chapter 12 above.

19. 2000 Act, s.71 (1)(a) & (3)(b)(i). See Chapter 9 above.

20. 2000 Act, s.71 (1) (b).

21. 2000 Act, s.71 (3) (b) (ii) & (iii) and (4).

22. 2000 Act, s.73 (1) & (3). See Chapter 16 below for circumstances where the public guardian considers that an adult's affairs can be properly protected by means of an authority to intromit. MWCS can only exercise the recall power where guardianship powers were granted on the basis of the adult's incapacity by reason of "mental disorder" (2000 Act, s.73 (3A)).

23. 2000 Act, s.73 (5).

24. 2000 Act, s.73 (7).

25. 2000 Act, s.73 (8) & (9). A modified procedure for recall of guardianship powers held by a local authority's CSWO is set out in 2000 Act, s.73. See also Chapter 15 below.

26. 2000 Act, s.72 (1).

27. 2000 Act, s.72 (2).

28. 2000 Act s.72 (3) – (6). See also Chapter 15 below.

29. In *Application in Re M* 2012 SLT (Sh Ct) 25, the default period of three years was considered to be more consistent with the CRPD (See Chapter 24 below). The view also was expressed that Courts should avoid awarding guardianship orders for an indefinite period under the relevant powers.

30. Criminal Procedure (Scotland) Act 1999, ss.57 & 58A. See also SAR, r.3.16.8 (1ZA) & (4).

# CHAPTER FOURTEEN

# INTERVENTION ORDERS

Intervention orders can be regarded as conferring authority on a person ("the intervener") to conduct the affairs of an incapable adult on a more targeted and specific basis than available under a guardianship order, and in a manner which is less restrictive of an adult's ability to exercise their legal agency. An intervention order can confer financial and property and / or welfare powers in favour of the intervener [1].

Why an Intervention order?

In order for an intervention order to be granted, the first question to be determined is whether the adult is "incapable". This question will require to be resolved by examination of the adult by suitably qualified medical practitioners [2]. On the basis this question is answered in the affirmative, the following tests may be appropriate:-

(i) Do the adult's circumstances require guardianship to be sought, if tested against the five principles?

(ii) If the situation requires a finite duration and specific purpose in order for it to be resolved, does an intervention order offer a better outcome?

(iii) Might granting of an intervention order, for example, resolve a conflict of interest in a specific area experienced by the adult's attorney or guardian?

As is specified in relation to other orders, any person (including the adult) claiming an interest in the "property, financial affairs or personal welfare" of an adult is entitled to apply for an intervention order [3].

The test for granting an intervention order is that:-

> "The adult is incapable of taking the action, or is incapable in relation to the decision about his property, financial affairs or personal welfare" [4].

Local authorities have power under to:-

> "investigate any circumstances made known to them in which the personal welfare of an adult seems to be at risk" [5].

In certain circumstances, the local authority is required to apply for an intervention order, where:-

> "it appears to the local authority that—
>
> (a) the adult is incapable as mentioned in subsection (1); and
>
> (b) no application has been made or is likely to be made for an order under this section in relation to the decision to which the application under this subsection relates; and
>
> (c) an intervention order is necessary for the protection of the property, financial affairs or personal welfare of the adult [6].

Much of the procedure for obtaining an intervention order transposes from the regime for obtaining a guardianship order [7]. This applies requirements relating to the provision of medical and MHO reports, and where the application relates only to the property and financial affairs of the adult, a report by a person who has "sufficient knowledge" to report on the appropriateness of the order sought and the suitability of the nominated intervener [8]. As a result, the prescribed forms requiring to be completed are the same as for a guardianship order [9].

It should be kept in mind that the Court retains an inherent power to appoint a safeguarder or *curator ad litem* to the adult, both for applications at first instance, and for and appeals [10]. The L&B practice note requires the solicitor acting for the applicant for an intervention order to send a copy of the application and relevant accompanying reports any answers to a safeguarder or *curator ad litem* within two working days of their appointment [11].

Where an intervention order is granted by the Sheriff, any action taken by the person so authorised:-

> "shall have the same effect as if done by the adult if he had the capacity to do so" [12].

In *Ward Appellant* [13], SP Kerr affirmed that the views of an incapacitated person as to who should inherit their estate on death, were "past and present wishes" of the adult having capacity at the time. In the instant case, there was no sufficient reason in principle why these should not be given effect via an intervention order authorising the adult's solicitor to execute a will on the adult's behalf, in accordance with the term of a previous draft will [14]. The Sheriff Principal also stated that the Sheriff had fallen into error in accepting the views of a MHO regarding the adult's testamentary capacity when the question essentially was one for a medically qualified practitioner [15].

Standing the manner in which an intervention order is expressed, in general, the order should not create the same scope for divesting agency from an adult to the extent that a guardianship order usually achieves. It is important to appreciate that the Sheriff may consider an application for the latter to be unjustified or unduly restrictive, and the Court may grant an intervention order instead on the basis, for example, of its being a "less restrictive [measure]" [16].

Possible tests for assessing the appropriateness of an intervention order may include:-

What is the adult's current situation regarding personal welfare and/or property and financial affairs?

- What needs of the adult are *not* being met and what changes should be made to the current situation to take account of the adult's needs?

- Would the adult want the intervention, if capable?

- Has the adult sufficient capacity to take decisions and to take action him or herself to meet these needs?

- Is there anyone already authorised to take the necessary decisions or action on behalf of the adult? If there is such a person or persons, is he or she, or are they, able and willing to take the necessary decisions or action?

- Are there any concerns with regard to anyone who has been appointed to exercise the powers?

What can an intervention order do?

An intervention order can direct the taking of any action specified by its terms. It can also authorise the person specified in the intervention order to take such action or make any decision specified (or both) [17]. Moreover, anything done under an intervention order shall have the same effect as if done by the adult as if they had the capacity to do so [18].

Where an intervention order directs the acquisition of accommodation for an adult, or the disposal of any accommodation used as a dwellinghouse by the adult, the consent of the public guardian is required as regards the proposed consideration of the transaction [19]. Where an intervention order relates to the property or financial affairs of the adult, the Sheriff is entitled to require the finding of caution or some other security as thought fit [20].

Where an intervention order has been made, the Sheriff can, on an application by the intervener, the adult, or "any person claiming an interest in the property, financial affairs or personal welfare of the adult", make a further order varying or recalling the terms of the intervention order [21]. When an intervention order is made, the Court is required to notify the public guardian, who will enter this in the public register, and issue a certificate of appointment to the intervener when satisfied that caution or any other appropriate security has been found [22].

Where an intervention order has been made which vests in the intervener a right to deal with, convey or manage any interest in heritable property, its terms must specify any property which forms part of the order [23]. The intervener is required to apply "forthwith" for the registration or recording of the relative intervention order in the land register or Register of Sasines [24].

An intervener must advise the public guardian, the local authority and, where the intervention order relates to the adult's welfare, and their incapacity results from a "mental disorder" the MWCS, of any change of address of the intervener or adult within seven days of this occurring [25]. The death of an intervener similarly requires to be notified to the public guardian by the personal representatives of the intervener if aware of the existence of the authority [26].

An intervener is entitled to recover any reasonable outlays incurred in carrying out the terms of the intervention order from the adult's estate [27]. An intervener is required to keep records of the exercise of their powers [28].

It is worth keeping in mind that the *code of practice* stresses that

> "Where the person's affairs are moderately complex or uncertain, intervention orders might prove to be insufficient to secure the necessary benefits and a guardianship order may be more suitable" [29].

## What can an intervention order do?

As with guardianship orders, there are few specific boundaries set by the 2000 Act as to what might form part of an intervention order. In the case of a financial intervention order, filling gaps left in a financial guardianship order or continuing power of attorney may often prove to be the purpose of an application. However, using an intervention order so as to consolidate an adult's bank accounts, wind up a business, or freeze assets pending completion of an investigation of financial issues are other evident possibilities.

In the case of a welfare intervention order, the making or requiring an adult to attend a medical appointment or assessment, or to arrange some form of care package or respite care may be amongst measures sought. It may be particularly important to consider the proportionality of the intervention sought, given its potential direct impact on an adult.

The *code of practice* recommends prior consultation with the local authority and/or MWCS prior to applying for an intervention order [30].

The making of an application for an intervention order has the effect of freezing authority for the carrying out of any medical treatment comprehended in the application:-

> "unless it is authorised by any other enactment or rule of law for the preservation of the life of the adult, or the prevention of serious deterioration in [their] condition" [31].

The "other enactment provision cannot apply where an interdict prohibiting the giving of such treatment is in effect. [32]

## Completion of an intervention order

On completion of the remit of an intervention order, an intervener does not require to obtain a discharge from the public guardian. However, where financial powers have been granted, progress reports of any dealings carried out require to submitted in order to be reviewed by the public guardian. Failure to do so can result in the matter being reported to the Sheriff Court. The process of providing accounts to the public guardian may occur more than once while an intervention order is in force [33].

Supervision by the local authority of the conduct of the intervention order can be ordered by the Sheriff. A local authority can act under s.13ZA of the Social Work (Scotland) Act 1968 to provide community care services, and the kind of circumstances where an intervention order may be useful in obtaining the appropriate level of services are considered later [34].

## NOTES (CHAPTER 14)

1. 548 Intervention orders were registered with the public guardian in 2023/24. Only 2 orders had welfare powers solely, and 1 contained both forms of powers.

2. See Chapter 8 above.

3. 2000 Act, s.53 (1).

4. 2000 Act, s.53 (1).

5. 2000 Act, s.10 (1) (d).

6. 2000 Act, s. 53 (3).

7. 2000 Act, s.53 (4).

8. See Chapter 9 above.

9. SAR, rr. 3.16.1 – 7. See Chapter 9 above. The L&B practice note applies the relevant parts of its terms to applications for intervention orders on the same basis as applications for guardianship orders.

10. See Chapter 15 below in relation to appeals.

11. L&B practice note, paras.3 (aa) and 4 (l).

12. 2000 Act, s.53 (9). As part of the process of considering the application, the Sheriff must have regard to any previous guardianship order or intervention order granted in relation to the adult (s.53 (2)).

13. 2014 SLT (Sh.Ct.) 15.

14. At para.5.

15. At para.17.

16. See *D v Falkirk Council 2023 GWD 10 – 110* at para.123. Nevertheless, the removal of agency from the Adult effected by the terms of the Intervention Order appears to have the same effect as comprehended by a Guardianship Order (See Chapter 9 above.

17. 2000 Act, s.53 (5).

18. 2000 Act, s.53 (9).

19. 2000 Act, s.53 (6).

20. 2000 Act, s.53 (7). See Chapter 9 above.

21. 2000 Act, s.53 (8).

22. 2000 Act, s.53 (10). The persons requiring to be notified are specified in s.53 (10) (b).

23. 2000 Act s.55.

24. 2000 Act, s.56A.

25. 2000 Act, s.53 (12).

26. 2000 Act, s.54. See Chapter 13 above.

27. *Code of practice*, para.2.3.

28. OPG Website. The *code of practice* advises consultation with the public guardian prior to seeking a financial intervention order (para.2.8). (See also Chapter 11 above).

29. *Code of practice*, para.2.3.

30. *Code of practice*, para.2.17.

31. 2000 Act, s.49 (1) & (2).

32. 2000 Act, s.49 (3).

33. 2000 Act, s.6 (2)(c)(iii).

34. See Chapter 21 below.

# CHAPTER FIFTEEN

# APPEALS IN RELATION TO GUARDIANSHIP ORDERS AND INTERVENTION ORDERS

It is important to understand the context in which Appeals under the Adults with Incapacity (Scotland) Act 2000 can be made. The 2000 Act provides that:-

> "Unless otherwise expressly provided for, any decision of the sheriff at first instance in any application to, or in any other proceedings before, him under this Act may be appealed to the sheriff principal, and the decision upon such appeal of the sheriff principal may be appealed, with the leave of the sheriff principal, to the Court of Session [1].

However, that provision must be read against changes effected by the Courts Reform (Scotland) Act 2014 ("the 2014 Act") which, amongst other matters, abolished any right of appeal from a decision of a Sheriff in civil proceedings to the Sheriff Principal [2]. In place of the existing right of appeal, the 2014 Act has created a counterpart right of appeal to the Sheriff Appeal Court.

Accordingly, the right created by s.2 (3) of the 2000 Act requires to be read in accordance with a provision that:-

> "any provision of any pre-commencement enactment that—
>
> (a) provides for an appeal to the sheriff principal from any decision of a sheriff in civil proceedings, or
>
> (b) restricts or excludes any such appeal.

> ......has effect as if for the reference to the sheriff principal there were substituted a reference to the Sheriff Appeal Court." [3]

It is submitted that this wording means that any decision made by a Sheriff in relation to any matter which comes them under the 2000 Act can be made the subject of appeal to the Sheriff Appeal Court, without the need to obtain permission [4]. Standing the wording of s.2 (3) of the 2000 Act, the Sheriff Appeal Court is entitled expressly to review any decisions of a Sheriff, other than those stated to be "final" as is considered below.

The relevant procedural rules are set out in the Act of Sederunt (Sheriff Appeal Court Rules) 2015 ("the SAC rules"). Amongst matters specified in the SAC rules is a requirement that an appeal must be made within 28 days of the date on which the decision appealed was given [5]. The matters requiring to be set out in a note of Appeal are specified in SAC rules, r.6.2. In determining an Appeal, the Sheriff Appeal Court is invested with a wide range of possible disposals, including recall or variation of the original decision, remit back to the Sheriff or adherence to the original decision [6].

Further Appeal from the Sheriff Appeal Court to the Court of Session is competent, with the permission of either Court where:-

(a) the appeal would raise an important point of principle or practice, or

(b) there is some other compelling reason for the Court of Session to hear the appeal" [7].

In *JK v Argyll and Bute Council* [8], the Sheriff Appeal Court confirmed that Appeals against its decisions under the 2000 Act can only be made under s.2 of the 2000 Act and not by means of s.113 of the Courts Reform (Scotland) Act 2014. Consequently, the procedure for obtaining Leave to Appeal is as expressed in s.2 (3) of the 2000 Act and could not be obtained directly from the Court of Session [9] Accordingly, the test applicable was the general test for Leave to Appeal [10].

The Sheriff Appeal Court is also entitled to remit matters to the Court of Session on the application of a party to an Appeal, where the Sheriff Appeal Court is satisfied that the Appeal "raises a complex or novel point of law" [11].

Of itself however, the 2014 Act does not address whether decisions of a Sheriff made under the 2000 Act which are stated to be "final" are themselves appealable under the 2014 Act. In principle, a "finality" clause is considered to exclude an appeal on the merits of a decision made by a Sheriff subject to such a provision [12]. On the other hand, where some form of procedural irregularity on the part of the Sheriff is argued, authority exists to the effect that an appeal to the Sheriff Appeal Court should be competent.

The Court of Session retains a jurisdiction exercising supervisory control over proceedings in the Sheriff Court [13]. It remains debatable whether such powers can properly exercised by means of an appeal as opposed to a judicial review, and there is acknowledged to be a dearth of recent authority on the question [14]. However, it is submitted that means exist to challenge decisions made under the 2000 Act which are made on an erroneous basis in law, if not in fact, even where such decisions are described as being "final" in nature.

A decision by any person other than a Sheriff as to the "incapacity" of an adult can be the subject of appeal [15].

## NOTES (CHAPTER 15)

1. 2000 Act, s.2 (3).

2. 2022 SC 235.

3. Courts Reform Act 2014, s.110.

4. 2014 Act, s.109 (2) & (3).

5. c.f 2014 Act, s.110.

6. SAC rules, r.6.3. See also r.1.3 regarding calculation of time periods.

7. 2014 Act, s.111 (1).

8. 2022 SC 235.

9. At Para.11. (See Courts Reform (Scotland) Act 2014, s.109 (2) & (3)).

10. At Para.12. See also *Boyle v Denton* [2024] SAC (Civ) 34 at para.11.

11. 2014 Act, s.113. See SAC rules, r.11, regarding applications for permission to Appeal to the Court of Session.

12. 2014 Act, s.112. See SAC rules, r.10.

13. MacPhail, *Sheriff Court Practice* (3rd Edition) (W. Green and Son), para.26.33.

14. *Brown v Hamilton District Council* 1983 SC (HL) 1.

15. See, for example, *Edinburgh North Constituency Association SNP Club v Thomas H Peck and Ors* 1978 SLT (Sh. Ct.) 76.

16. 2000 Act, s.14.

# CHAPTER SIXTEEN

# OTHER FINANCIAL MANAGEMENT ARRANGEMENTS

The 2000 Act provides a number of arrangements for the management of the funds of an incapable adult, which can be authorised by the public guardian. Their scope is considerably less than will be comprehended by a guardianship order or intervention order. (It should be noted that some of the provisions considered below may be superseded by proposals under consideration by the review of mental health law in Scotland [1]).

However, in accordance with the principle of applying the least restrictive option to an adult [2] such arrangements may be all that is required to ensure the proper use and management of an adult's funds. However, it is not possible to make application for any of the orders considered in this Chapter where an adult is subject to guardianship or intervention order, or has a continuing attorney with powers relating to their funds [3]. In practice, however, resort to the authority to intromit process is relatively sparing in practice [4].

In order for any of the applications considered in the section of this Chapter concerned with authority to intromit, an adult must be "incapable" in relation to decisions about, or safeguarding the adult's interests in, the funds in question [5]. This requires a certificate from a "medical practitioner" that the adult is incapable of meeting one or both of the following criteria:-

> "[X] is incapable in relation to decisions about or incapable of acting to safeguard or promote his/her interests in his or her funds. [by reason of mental disorder or inability to communicate]" [6]

An applicant for any of the orders relating to authority to intromit can be an individual or a statutory body – including a local authority – or a voluntary organisation or charity [7]. Any of the applications specified in s.27A (1) of the 2000 Act which are made by an individual require to be countersigned by someone who has known the applicant for at least a year prior to the making of the application [8]. The public guardian can disapply requirements for provision of a medical certificate and/ or counter signature of an application where an application already has been made for one of the authorisations made under sections 24C, 24D or 25 of the 2000 Act [9].

In determining any of the applications considered in this Chapter, the test applied by the public guardian in determining these is whether the applicant is "a fit and proper person to intromit with the funds of the adult" [10]. In so doing, the public guardian is required to have regard to any guidance issued by Scottish ministers relative to this test, as well as offer the opportunity for the applicant to make representations where the public guardian is minded to refuse an application [11].

Moreover, the public guardian is required to intimate an application to various specified parties [12], and cannot grant any application in relation to authority to intromit which have been intimated, without offering these parties the opportunity to object and to allow representations to be made [13].

Where the public guardian is entitled to remit such applications to the Sheriff for determination, whose decision on the application is "final" [14].

## A: AUTHORITY TO INTROMIT

Authority to operate the bank or building society accounts of an adult can be obtained from the public guardian via the authority to intromit (also described as "access to funds") procedure. This is described as a "simplified and limited form of financial guardianship", which has the potential to supersede the need for financial guardianship.

The public guardian can grant authority for a prospective applicant to initiate management of the adult's funds by:-

- Obtaining information from a fundholder (bank, building society or similar body) in support of the application for authority to intromit [15].

- Opening an account in the adult's name for the purpose of intromitting with the adult's funds where there is not already a "suitable account" for the purpose in the adult's sole name [16].

These steps may be a precursor to an application for authority to intromit or for the purposes of allowing funds to be transferred. The information can also be sought simultaneously with an application for authority to intromit, if details of the account are provided to the public guardian.

When an application for authority to intromit is made to the public guardian, the purposes of the authority sought are specified as being:-

> "(a) the payment of central and local government taxes for which the adult is responsible;
>
> (b) the provisions of sustenance, accommodation, fuel, clothing and related goods and services for the adult;
>
> (c) the provision of other services provided for the purposes of looking after or caring for the adult;
>
> (d) the settlement of debts owed by or incurred in respect of the adult, including any prescribed fees charged by the public guardian in connection with an application under this Part;
>
> (e) the payment for the provision of items other than those mentioned in paragraphs (a) to (d) such as the public guardian may, in any case, authorise." [17].

Beyond providing information regarding the adult and the proposed holder of the authority to intromit, the application to the public guardian will also contain:-

- A statement of the purposes of the intromission with the adult's funds proposed expenditure (including particulars of regular expenditure) on behalf of the adult [18].

- An undertaking to open an identified "designated account" for the purposes of receiving funds from "the adult's current account" and for intromitting with the funds. The applicant may also seek to open a "second account" in the adult's name for that purpose [19].

Where the public guardian grants an application to intromit with funds, this is entered into the public register, and a document (a "withdrawal certificate") is then issued to the applicant. The holder of the withdrawal certificate is termed "the withdrawer". A withdrawal certificate can authorise the transfer of funds from the adult's "current account" to the "designated account; the "current account" to the "second account"; and the "designated account" to the "second account" [20]. A transfer of funds which would cause one or more of these accounts to become overdrawn is not authorised by a withdrawal certificate [21]. In that event, the fundholder of the account has a right of relief against the withdrawer [22].

A withdrawal certificate can also:-

> "(b) authorise the continuance or making of arrangements for the regular or occasional payment of funds from the adult's current account for specified purposes (for example: by standing order or direct debit);
>
> (c) authorise the withdrawal of funds from the designated account for specified purposes;

(d) place limits on the amount of funds that may be so transferred, paid or withdrawn." [23].

In day-to-day terms therefore, the adult's funds under management become ringfenced.

The withdrawer should then be able to manage the adult's accounts, obtain a cash card or cheque book and arrange internet banking.

A withdrawal certificate will normally run for a period of three years from the date of issue, albeit the period can be reduced or extended by the public guardian, including making the period without limit of time [26]. A decision on the period of a withdrawal certificate can be appealed to the Sheriff, whose decision on the matter is "final" [27]. The terms of a withdrawal certificate can be varied by the public guardian where sought by the withdrawer, or in response to notification of change of address of the adult or withdrawer [28].

In addition, a withdrawer or person applying for authority to intromit can seek authority to transfer a specified sum from the "original account" to any of the three accounts previously mentioned, or "such other account as may be specified". This may also seek closure of the "original account" or terminate arrangements for payment of funds from that account by means, for example, of standing orders or direct debits [29].

The public guardian is entitled to suspend or withdraw the authority of the withdrawal certificate. This had the effect of terminating all operations on the designated account, although the public guardian can also grant at this point an interim withdrawal certificate which allows the withdrawer to continue to intromit with the adult's funds for a maximum period of four weeks [30]. A decision to suspend or terminate authority by this means can be appealed to the Sheriff, whose decision on the matter is "final" [31]. The public guardian is also entitled to cancel a withdrawal certificate within its originally specified period [32].

Renewal of a withdrawal certificate can be made by the holder of an existing withdrawal certificate, or where a main withdrawer has designed or become incapable or had their authority terminated, and application is made "without undue delay" by a then reserve withdrawer. In the former case, the withdrawal certificate remains in force until the renewal application is determined. The public guardian can disapply the requirements for submission of forms, and require provide any information needed to determine the application [33].

A withdrawer is required to keep a record of the exercise of their powers. The public guardian can make enquiries from time to time regarding the conduct of the withdrawer's authority [34]. The public guardian is entitled to require a withdrawer to provide the records of their exercise of their functions and any other information reasonably required in relation to an investigation or inquiry [35].

The responsibilities and liability of any fundholder – that is a bank, building society or other similar body which holds funds on behalf of another person [36] – of an original account, current account or second account are specified in the 2000 Act, ss.28, 28A and 29.

A withdrawer must apply funds "only for the benefit of the adult" except in the case of a cohabitee, who may apply funds to household expenses to the extent authorised by the withdrawal certificate [37]. For holders of joint accounts, specific provision is made that in the event of one holder becoming incapable of operating the account, any other joint account holder can continue to operate it in the absence of a specific provision in the account or any court order preventing this from happening [38].

The public guardian is empowered to receive and investigate complaints regarding the exercise of functions the financial affairs concerning intromissions made under the withdrawal of funds provisions [39].

## B: MANAGEMENT OF RESIDENTS' FINANCES

In the particular circumstances of individuals residing in hospitals or care homes who lack capacity to manage their finances, it is possible for the managers of the establishment to be authorised to become responsible for:-

> "(a) claiming, receiving, holding and spending any pension, benefit, allowance or other payment other than expressly excluded;
>
> (b) claiming, receiving, holding and spending any money to which a resident is entitled;
>
> (c) holding any other moveable property to which the resident is entitled;
>
> (d) disposing of such moveable property [40].

The "incapacity" of a resident for this purpose is established by a process beginning with the managers arranging examination of the resident by a medial practitioner who, if so satisfied, can issue a certificate in a prescribed form [41]. A certificate relating to a resident expires 3 years after it is granted, but can be reviewed in the event of there being a "change in the condition of circumstances...bearing on the resident's incapacity" [42].

Where the managers propose to exercise the statutory process, they are required to send a copy of the certificate to the resident and to the "supervisory body" of their establishment [43] along with notice of their intention manage the resident's affairs. [44].

Authorisation of withdrawal from an account or source of funds of a resident flows from a certificate of authority issued by the "supervisory body", which must specify the staff at an establishment ("authorised person") and the accounts or funds which can be managed. The period of validity of the authority must of the authorisation must also be stated [45]

The authorised managers will require to operate subject to the five principles of the 2000 Act, and also are required to "act only for the benefit of the resident". The extent of authority is to manage the disposal of and item or items of moveable property up to the value of £100 or £10,000 in relation to any other matter [46].

The managers are required to maintain separate funds and individual records of the stewardship of the resident's funds, including the keeping of records. They also must be able to track the funds received by the resident and to account for allocation of any interest accrued. A statement of affairs of the resident requires to be prepared as at the date when a resident ceases to be incapable, and where the resident moves to another establishment or elsewhere, unless the resident has ceased to be incapable [47].

Where a former resident has ceased to be incapable or ceases to reside in the establishment, the managers of the original establishment can continue to manage the resident's affairs until other arrangements are made, for a period of up to three months [48]. At the end of this period, the managers are required to prepare a statement to be given to the former resident, if capable, or to any person assuming responsibility for managing their affairs [49].

The managers should spend the money they are authorised to deal with only on items and services "of benefit to the [resident]", further defined to mean not spending money on services normally provided by the establishment as part of its normal service. The managers should maintain insurance indemnifying the resident against any loss arising from their management of the funds [50].

Authority to manage a resident's funds can only be obtained where the adult already does not have a financial guardian, a person exercising financial powers under a power of attorney or "other person with powers relating to that matter" [51].

The "supervisory body" of an establishment is entitled to revoke a management power where it considers that the establishment is not operating, or is not complying with the authorisation and the relevant part of the 2000 Act, or otherwise that it is no longer appropriate that it should manage residents affairs. Such revocation takes effect 14 days after notification, after which the "supervisory body" assumes responsibility for management of the residents' affairs, pending transfer to another person [52].

Any decision by the "supervisory body" can be appealed to the Sheriff whose decision is described as "final" [53]. Complaints regarding discharge of the power to manage a resident's finances will be directed to the care commission or local health board, according to the nature of the establishment concerned.

The Scottish Government is consulting on abolition of management of residents' finances and its incorporation into a proposed graded guardianship regime [54].

## C: APPOINTEE TO COLLECT SOCIAL SECURITY BENEFITS

Circumstances will arise where the sole source of income of an adult with incapacity will be social security benefits such as the retirement pension or PiP / ADP. Accordingly, where the adult does not have a financial guardian in place, and the claimant is "unable to act" in relation to their benefits, it is possible to nominate a person over 18 who can be appointed to receive and deal with the benefits.

Following an application to the DWP, the department can decide to pay a benefit in whole or in part to "another person acting on behalf of the claimant" if necessary to protect the interests of the claimant or any children and dependants [55].

## NOTES (CHAPTER 16)

1. See Chapter 24 below.

2. See Chapter 3 above.

3. 2000 Act, s.24B. See Chapter 2 above in relation to an adult's "incapacity". The public guardian can initiate the recall of a guardianship order (See Chapter 14 above) where satisfied that granting an authority to intromit can satisfactorily "safeguard or promote the adult's interest in their property and affairs" (s.31E).

4. 194 authorities to intromit were issued by the public guardian in 2023-24, as opposed to 364 in 2013-14, reflecting an historic downwards trend. The *Review of Mental Health Law in Scotland* proposed the replacement of the Access to Funds regime, but at the time of writing, the Scottish Government is consulting on a modified and simplified scheme of Access to Funds, where supervision would be exercised by the OPG in a manner similar to that applying to Financial Guardianship.

5. 2000 Act, s.24B.

6. 2000 Act, s.27B

7. 2000 Act, s.25(2).

8. 2000 Act, s.27A (1). The form of the certificate is specified in the Schedule to the Adults with Incapacity (Accounts and Funds) (Scotland) Regulations 2008.

9. 2000 Act, s.27F.

10. 2000 Act, s.27D (1).

11. 2000 Act, s.27D(2).

12. 2000 Act, s.27C.

13. 2000 Act, s.27E.

14. 2000 Act, s.27F. A refusal by the public guardian to remit an application to the Sheriff can itself be subject to Appeal (s.31D (1)(b)). See Chapter 15 above in relation to decisions of the Sheriff stated to be "final".

15. 2000 Act, s.24C.

16. 2000 Act, s.24D. The details of the proposed account(s) which require to be notified to the public guardian are set out in the Adults with Incapacity (Accounts and Funds) (Scotland) Regulations 2008, regn.2. See also *W v Office of the Public Guardian 2010 GWD 27- 560.*

17. 2000 s.24A.

18. 2000 Act, s.26(1)(a).

19. 2000 Act, s.26(1)–(3).

20. 2000 Act, s.26A (1).

21. 2000 Act, s.26A (2).

22. 2000 Act, s.26A (3).

23. 2000 Act, s.26A (1) (b)-(d).

24. 2000 Act, s.27D (1).

25. 2000 Act, ss.27D (2) & 27E.

26. 2000 Act, s.31 (1) & (2).

27. 2000 Act, s.31D.

28. 2000 Act, ss.26F & 30A. Arrangements can also be made for the appointment of a joint or reserve withdrawer (ss.26B – 26E).

29. 2000 Act, s.26G (1)-(3).

30. 2000 Act, s.31A.

31. 2000 Act, s31 (1) (d). See FN 9 above.

32. 2000 Act, s.31C (2). This decision is not capable of appeal to the Sheriff under s.31D of the 2000 Act, presumably because the public guardian would only exercise the power at the request of the withdrawer.

33. 2000 Act, s.31B

34. 2000 Act, s.30B (1). See Chapter 17 below. In this case, the emphasis of records is likely to be financial, combined with explanation of any decisions to expend funds.

35. 2000 Act, s.81A (1)(a) & 2 (b). See also ss.6(2) (c) & (d) and s.30B (2). Similar powers exist in relation to any person who holds (or has held) funds on behalf for an adult (s.81A (1) (b) & (3)).

36. 2000 Act, s.33 (2).

37. 2000 Act, s.30.

38. 2000 Act, s.32.

39. 2000 Act, s.6 (2)(c)(iii). See Chapter 17 below.

40. 2000 Act, s.39 (1). In relation to head (d) the managers are required to "have regard" to the sentimental value an item might have for a resident, or would have, but for their incapacity (s.39 (2) (b)). This process also applies to persons whose detention is authorised under the Criminal Procedure (Scotland) Act 1995 or

the Mental Health (Care and Treatment) (Scotland) Act 2003 (2000 Act, s.35 (5)). The Scottish Government has proposed the abolition of the Management of Residents Finances regime.

41. 2000 Act, s.37 (2). The form of the certificate is set out in the Adults with Incapacity (Management of Residents Finances) (No.2) Regulations 2003, Sched.2. Notice of an intention to conduct such an examination must be sent to the resident and also to their "nearest relative" and "named person" (s.37 (3). (See Chapter 4 above. See also s.37 (6) in relation to conflict of interest by the certifier and Chapter 2 above).

42. 2000 Act, s.37 (7). The "supervisory body" is responsible for transmission of the certificate and notice of intention to manage the resident's affairs to their "nearest relative" and "named person" (s.37 (4)).

43. See 2000 Act, s.40.

44. The notice of intention to manage the resident's funds must specify what other courses of action were considered and why they were not considered appropriate (s.37 (5)).

45. 2000 Act, s.42 (1)–(3).

46. 2000 Act, s.39 (2) & (3). The figures quoted are those prescribed by the Adults with Incapacity (Management of Residents Finances) (No.2) (Scotland) Regulations 2003, which have not been increased since these Regulations were made. It is possible for the "supervisory body" of the managers to authorise a higher figure.

47. 2000 Act, s.43.

48. 2000 Act, s.44 (1).

49. 2000 Act, s.44 (2).

50. 2000 Act, s.41.

51. 2000 Act, s.46. The wider description is most likely to be applicable to a person holding powers under an intervention order.

52. 2000 Act, s.45 (1)-(4). A revocation of authority can itself be annulled by the "supervisory body" (s.45 (5)).

53. 2000 Act, s.45 (6). See Chapter 15 above, regarding a decision of the Sheriff which is stated to be "final".

54. See Chapter 24 below.

55. Social Security (Claims and Payments) Regulations 1987, regns. 33 & 34). Similar arrangements can also be made in relation to matters such as national savings Social Security (Claims and Payments) Regulations 1987, regns.33 & 34). Similar arrangements can also be made in relation to matters such as national savings certificates, premium bonds etc. (See *Agents, Appointees Attorneys and Deputies Guide* (DWP) generally).

# CHAPTER SEVENTEEN

# SUPERVISION AND WHEN THINGS GO WRONG

Reference has been made above to situations where a professional individual often may be appointed to act for an adult with incapacity under a power of attorney or guardianship order. A failure to discharge these responsibilities in an adequate manner may lay such an individual open to regulatory action by their profession, which essentially lies beyond the scope of this work.

However, it very often may be the case that a lay individual – most usually a member of the adult's family or close friend – assumes the responsibility under such orders, and thus the scope for honest error or misjudgement may be greater as a consequence. Advice and assistance can be obtained from professional sources, but for a lay person, other primary sources of supervision and support may be found in the public guardian, the local authority for the area in which an adult is "habitually resident" and the MWCS.

Reference will be made in this Chapter to various provisions in which the aforementioned statutory bodies exercise powers of supervision or enforcement. However, the *Codes of practice* referred to in earlier parts of the text contain extensive pointers to stages where consultation with, or obtaining of advice from these bodies is recommended. In appropriate instances, such referrals may be applicable to lay and professional actors alike.

## Public guardian

An important aspect of the public guardian's role is supervision of the conduct of financial guardianships, and the prevention of misuse or dissipation of an adult's funds. Accordingly, sets of accounts must be submitted by financial guardians on a regular basis to the public guardian.

The first set of accounts must be submitted 18 months from the first registration of the guardianship order and then annually, together with related information [1]. The public guardian will approve accounts where they appear to provide "a true and fair view of the financial guardian's management of the adult's estate". This furnishes the public guardian with a wide discretion, which can be exercised so as to disregard "minor inconsistencies" and absence of documents, if satisfied that the financial guardian acted "reasonably and in good faith" [2].

Where the public guardian has concerns regarding the accounts and/or supporting information furnished by, it can issue a report to a financial guardian, outlining where the accounts appear to fail to provide a "true and fair view". It is open to the guardian to object to any parts of the report, and ultimately disputes can be resolved by means of a reference the Sheriff [3].

It should be noted that a specific requirement of the public guardian is that where the value of moveable estate of an adult exceeds £25,000, the financial guardian must obtain professional advice on the management and application of the funds [4]. Failure to follow this advice potentially may reflect a failure to apply the fiduciary duty and duty of care applying to a financial guardian [5].

The public guardian is entitled to fix both the remuneration due to a financial guardian [6] and the amount of outlays incurred to be reimbursed to both a financial guardian and welfare guardian [7]. Remuneration by way of payments to account may also be authorised by the public guardian in the course of an "accounting period" [8]. A decision of the public guardian as to the amount of outlays or remuneration authorised can be appealed to the Sheriff, whose decision on such matters is "final" [9].

Where a guardian is found to have been in breach of any duty of care, fiduciary duty or obligation, the Sheriff may order the forfeiture of the whole or part of the guardian's remuneration, on the application of anyone with an interest in "the property, financial affairs or personal welfare" of an adult [10].

It should be noted that the powers referred to apply only to guardians and not to interveners, presumably on the basis that broad powers of investigation of the latter rest with the public guardian under the 2000 Act [11], and the duration of such an order is likely to be relatively short. As mentioned previously, the public guardian has a supervisory power to make enquiries into the exercise of withdrawal powers [12].

Local authority

A local authority has supervisory powers in relation to the conduct of a welfare power of attorney, welfare guardianship or intervention order [13]. Requirements are made by Regulations, specifying the periods during which either the office holder or the adult concerned should be visited [14].

In a case where a welfare guardianship has been granted, both the adult and the office holder should be visited within three months of the relevant order being granted, and thereafter at intervals of not more than twelve months [15]. Where an intervention order is being supervised, the local authority are required to visit the adult and the intervener as often as directed by the Sheriff in the order, or else at intervals of not more than one month while the order remains in force [16].

Where the circumstances of the adult concerned are such that it is not possible for the local authority to visit the adult within the specified time periods, such a visit must take place "as close to the time when the visit should have taken place, as the adult's circumstances will permit" [17]. Following the initial visits, the local authority may decide to extend the interval between visits to more than 12 months, or else cease visits completely [18]. Where this course is adopted, the local authority must notify the MWCS [19]. Such action cannot be taken where the adult or guardian objects to the proposal [20].

In the case of a welfare power of attorney, where the Sheriff has directed that the exercise of powers should be supervised [21], the local authority is required to visit the adult and the welfare attorney as often as specified by the Sheriff, and in the absence of such requirement, at least once a month [22].

In relation to any visits required by the Regulations, a visit by the local authority to the adult can take place at the same time as the visit to the office holder [23]. In each case, the local authority is entitled to require a report from the office holder relating to the personal welfare of the adult and the exercise of functions [24].

The statutory bodies

Each of the public guardian, MWCS and a local authority have powers under the 2000 Act to conduct investigations [25] where they consider that necessary in order to safeguard the property, financial affairs or personal welfare of an adult [26]. Each body is required to provide each other with "such information and assistance" as may be necessary to facilitate any investigation [27].

Personal liability

Any of the persons considered in this section; that is a financial or welfare attorney, guardian, intervener, withdrawer or manager of an establishment who use funds:-

(i) in breach of their fiduciary duty [28];

(ii) outwith their authority; or

(iii) after the termination of their authority

is liable to repay the funds to the adult [29].

What this provision leaves unclear is how an adult who is incapable is able to enforce the liability against the office holder. It is possible to envisage that a friend or relative might seek an intervention order, but the practicalities involved in obtaining the order [30] may render pursuit of small sums effectively uneconomic.

A financial guardian is liable to make good any deficiency in accounts approved by the public guardian. The public guardian also is empowered to require the payment of interest for the period during which the deficiency has occurred [31].

The relief provision

The 2000 Act provides that:

> "*No liability* shall be incurred by a guardian, financial attorney, welfare attorney, intervener, withdrawer or managers of an establishment for *any breach* of any duty of care or fiduciary duty owed to the adult if they have:-
>
> (a) acted reasonably and in good faith, and *in accord with the principles set out in Section 1.*
>
> (b) failed to act and the failure was reasonable *and in accord with the principles set out in Section 1* [32].

While there have not been any reported cases in which the import of s.82 (1) has been considered, it is submitted that a significant degree of latitude will be offered, given that two different individuals could assess some or all of the elements discussed in this chapter and come to diametrically opposed outcomes. What is more problematic potentially is a situation where no consideration whatsoever of the five principles has taken place, potentially for reasons of self – interest or conflict of interest.

It will be apparent that there is scope for liability to be avoided where some degree of care has been taken to manage the adult's property and funds. The simple fact that the officeholder made a mistake or acted or failed to act in a particular way does not necessarily attach liability. What is important however, is that the five principles can be shown to have been considered as part of the impugned process, alongside any guidance contained in a relevant *Code of practice*, or contained in advice from the public guardian and MWCS.

Thus, the purchase of a secondhand car by a financial guardian might well be shown to be motivated by the aim of allowing the adult greater freedom of movement and access to their family and friends. In essence, the potential benefit accruing justifies the expense. In the event that the car's engine seizes after 200 miles, rendering it valueless, the extent to which the financial guardian took care to check the condition of the vehicle might be relevant to establishing acting in good faith. If it was established that the financial guardian wished to have the vehicle for his or her use primarily, the benefit to the adult may seem more doubtful.

In practice, assessment of the use of funds by such an officeholder is likely to be viewed over a longer timeframe, and advice from the *Code of practice* and public guardian emphasise the critical nature of making and retaining records of actions taken and funds expended [33].

## Misuse of powers of attorney

Reference was made above to the financial liability which either a continuing or welfare attorney may incur under s.82 of the 2000 Act, and also to the investigatory powers of the public guardian, MWCS or local authority. Beyond that, the public guardian also has the ability to require production of records from a continuing attorney as part of conducting an investigation [34].

This represents the extent of non – criminal examination of the conduct of a power of attorney, and in many respects, such examination will arise from complaints made, as compared to the required regular scrutiny of accounts maintained by financial guardians. In England, the public guardian has increased the number of references made to the Court of

Protection in recent years. While the public guardian in Scotland also has powers to bring apparent abuse to the attention of the Sheriff Court [35], there is a tension between the freedom of the granter of a power of attorney to make arrangements satisfactory to them, and the role of the state in preventing exploitation of vulnerable individuals, which the current arrangements may not properly resolve.

## Criminal Law

Several issues of criminal law potentially arise in relation to adults with incapacity. The 2000 Act does not create any specific criminal offence of misusing funds while acting as one of the office holders who can be appointed under the 2000 Act, but such matters most likely would be treated most likely as offences of embezzlement or fraud.

An offence has been created of sexual abuse of trust by a person providing care services to a "mentally disordered person" [36]. It is also an offence for anyone exercising powers under the 2000 Act relating to the welfare of an adult to "ill-treat or wilfully neglect" the adult [37].

It should be kept in mind that while many of the civil matters outlined in this work can be found to be established on a balance of probabilities, the higher criminal standard of proof must be achieved before a criminal conviction will ensue.

## NOTES (CHAPTER 17)

1. 2000 Act, sched.2, para.7 (3).

2. 2000 Act, sched.2, para.8 (1) & (2).

3. 2000 Act, sched.2, paras.8 (1)(b) & (3)-(5).

4. Public guardian website.

5. See Chapter 11 above.

6. 2000 Act, s.68 (6). A financial guardian is entitled to remuneration unless, having considered the value of an adult's estate and the likely difficulty in managing it, the Sheriff directs otherwise in making the guardianship order (s.68 (4) & (5)). "Special cause" requires to be shown before a Sheriff can order remuneration to be paid to a welfare guardian (s.64 (4) (a)).

7. 2000 Act, s.68 (2) (a) (which defines "outlays") and (6). This assessment normally occurs where accounts are submitted by the financial guardian for auditing by the public guardian (s.68 (c). See also Chapter 15 above).

8. 2000 Act, s.68 (7).

9. 2000 Act, s.68 (8). See Chapter 15 above.

10. 2000 Act, s.69. No mechanism is expressly provided for reclaiming any remuneration forfeited by a guardian, but it is likely the Court would frame any order appropriately.

11. 2000 Act, s.6 (2)(b)(v) & (c) (iii).

12. See Chapter 16 above.

13. 2000 Act, s.10 (1) (a).

14. 2000 Act, s.10 (1) (c).

15. Adults with Incapacity (Supervision of Welfare Guardians etc. by Local Authorities) (Scotland) Regulations 2002, regn.2 (1).

16. 2002 Regulations, regn.2 (3).

17. 2002 Regulations, regn.2 (5).

18. 2002 Regulations, regn.2A (2).

19. 2002 Regulations, regn.2A (3). The local authority can also decide to resume visiting the adult and guardian (Regn.2A (5) & (6)).

20. 2002 Regulations, regn.2A (3).

21. 2000 Act, s.20 (2) (c).

22. Adults with Incapacity (Supervision of Welfare Attorneys by Local Authorities) (Scotland) Regulations 2001, regn.2 (1). The specified periods will not apply where it is "not possible" to visit the adult, albeit such visits should take place "as close to the [specified time] as the adult's circumstances will allow (Regn.5(5)).

23. 2001 Regulations, regn.2 (2); 2002 Regulations, regn.2 (4).

24. 2001 Regulations, regn.3; 2002 Regulations, regn.3 (a) and (b) (See also regn.3A).

25. See 2000 Act, s.6 (2) (Public Guardian); 2000 Act, s.9 (1) (MWCS); 2000 Act, s.10 (1) (Local authority). At the time of writing, the Scottish Government is consulting on how the division of responsibilities for investigations should be made between the public guardian and local authorities.

26. 2000 Act, s.12 (1).

27. 2000 Act, s.12 (2).

28. See Chapter 11 above.

29. 2000 Act, s.81.

30. See Chapter 14 above.

31. 2000 Act, schd.2, paras.8 (6) & (7).

32. 2000 Act, s.82 (Emphases added).

33. See Chapters 7, 11 & 14 above.

34. 2000 Act, s.81A. The power of the public guardian also applies to a guardian, and intervener and a withdrawer (See also s.30B (2)), and mention has been made elsewhere of supervision of welfare attorneys.

35. 2000 Act, s.6 (2) (da).

36. Sexual Offences (Scotland) Act, s.17 (2) & (3), which apply the definition of "mental disorder" provided by s.328 of the 2000 Act, is created under s.46 of the Sexual Offences (Scotland) Act 2009. Defences to the offence are specified in s.47.

37. 2000 Act, s.83. The Scottish Government has proposed that financial abuse of a vulnerable adult should be established as an additional crime.

# CHAPTER EIGHTEEN

# WHAT WILL IT COST?

Entering arrangements of a power of attorney will vary, depending partly upon the extent to which the granter intends to cede powers to their attorney, as well as the value and complexity of their assets, and the extent of welfare powers granted [1]. Ultimately, matters relating to the cost of administering the granter's estate, or where applicable, undertaking any steps necessary to advance the granter's welfare, will be a matter to be addressed in the power of attorney.

As far as applying for a guardianship order is concerned, in general the expenses of a successful application for an order to the Sheriff Court which are properly and reasonably incurred, will come from the adult's estate [2]. There is authority that such expenses should be assessed in an agent and client, client paying basis [3].

A statutory exception to this rule can arise where the public guardian, MWCS or local authority become parties to proceedings under the 2000 Act, in order to protect an adult's interests, where the Court can award expenses against the adult or against any person "whose actings have resulted in the proceedings" [4]. Where any of these bodies enter such proceedings in order to "represent the public interest", expenses may be awarded against any person whose actings have resulted in the proceedings or whose conduct has been unreasonable in relation thereto [5].

The extent to which an individual applying for a guardianship or intervention order may be eligible for legal aid or legal advice and assistance (LAA) requires careful consideration. The Scottish legal aid board (SLAB) which administers the legal aid scheme has issued guidance which states that LAA is available, subject to financial eligibility, based upon the adult's resources. Legal aid is provided where a guardianship order or intervention order is sought which contain welfare powers or welfare and financial powers, without a means test. Where only financial powers are sought, a means test based upon the resources of the adult will be applied, and a financial contribution may be applied.

Legal aid may also be made available, on the basis outlined, to enable opposition to be mounted to an application for a welfare guardianship or an intervention order. In relation to cases seeking legal aid, the solicitor making the application will require to be satisfied that the criterion of "reasonableness" applied by SLAB is likely to be met [6].

At the time of writing, the fees relative to certain orders sought under the 2000 Act are:-

- Summary application £141
- Minute £54
- Fixing a hearing £60
- Each day or part day hearing £256
- Lodging an Appeal to Sheriff Appeal Court £126

The fees of the public guardian [7] relative to a power of attorney are:-

- Submission of a power of attorney £87
- Deed of amendment £87
- Audit of accounts £135

The fees of the public guardian relative to guardianship orders are:-

- Registration of guardianship order/ Variation/ Renewal – £97

- Recall of guardianship order (Non-heritable) – £60
- Recall of guardianship order (with heritable property) – £135
- Inventory – £60 (£0 – £30,000) increasing in stages up to £1,363 (£500,001 and above).
- Initial audit and intermediate reviews – £90 (£0 – £30,000) increasing in stages to £1,090 (£500,001 and above).
- Final audit £169 (£0 – £30,000) increasing in stages to £1,172 (£500,001 and above).

For an intervention order

- Registration or variation – £97

As regards access to funds, the fees are:-

- Application to obtain information – £97
- Application for authority to access funds – £97
- Withdrawal certificate for joint/ reserve/substitute withdrawer – £70
- Transfer of specified sum – £20
- Renewal of withdrawal certificate – £55

## NOTES (CHAPTER 18)

1. On some websites, an indicative cost for a solicitor drafting a standard power of attorney of £200 – £350. In the *Code of practice for continuing and welfare attorneys* (Scottish Government) (2018) para.1.21, reference is made to the possible availability of Legal advice and assistance from the Scottish legal aid board (SLAB) in connection with powers of attorney. See FN7 below.

2. See *Galashan Applicant 2008 GWD 29 – 449.* The cost of an application by a local authority to appoint their CWSO as a financial guardian to an adult can be recovered from an adult's estate (2000 Act, s.68 (3)).

3. *H's Curator Bonis, Applicant 2010 SLT (Sh.Ct) 230.* There is no reported authority on how expenses should be awarded where an application is made for an intervention order, but it is submitted that the approach should be the same as applies to an application for a guardianship order.

4. 2000 Act, s.8 (1).

5. 2000 Act, s.8 (2).

6. *Adults with incapacity (Scotland) act 2000. Fact sheet. Legal aid (SLAB).* See also https://www.slab.org.uk/guidance/adults-with-incapacity-awi/ and *Code of practice for persons authorised under intervention orders and guardians* (Scottish Government) (2011), para.1.21.

7. Figures published on the public guardian website, effective from 1 April 2024.

# CHAPTER NINETEEN

# CONDUCTING TRANSACTIONS

Reference has been made to the powers which are vested in persons who hold offices carrying financial powers to conduct transactions on behalf of an incapable adult. For those who transact with such persons, there are certain aspects to the counterpart of such transactions which require consideration.

The authority of an attorney to act in terms of a power of attorney is terminated when the deed has been revoked by the granter, and notice has been registered by the public guardian [1]. Authority is also terminated by the resignation of the attorney [2], by the death of the granter [3], and by the appointment of a financial or welfare guardian to the granter conferring "powers relating to that matter" [4].

The authority of a person authorised to act under a guardianship order or intervention order can be terminated by a number of means [5]. Provision is also made for the termination of the authority of a person authorised to act under an authority to intromit [6].

In each case, it is likely that the office holder will enjoy a power to enter transactions of a greater or lesser nature, in accordance with the extent of powers conferred upon them by a power of attorney, guardianship or intervention order, or authority to intromit. However, that is a separate question to what happens where transactions are entered by an office holder who may be unaware of an adult's death, or a third party who has no reason to believe that the office holder's authority to transact has ended. The 2000 Act addresses the issue in a number of ways.

## Dealing with heritable property

Powers of attorney, financial guardianships and intervention orders can authorise dealing with the heritable property of an adult. Financial guardianship and intervention orders which contain such powers either will be recorded in the land register or endorsed in the General Register of Sasines [7].

Where title to heritable property passes from a continuing attorney, that title cannot be challenged on the basis alone that a purchaser has acted in good faith unaware of the termination of a power of attorney or the appointment of a financial guardian [8]. Such title also cannot be challenged where a third party has in good faith and for value acquired title from a financial guardian or intervener whose authority has been terminated or come to an end [9].

Similarly, such title to heritable property cannot not be challenged where a third party, acting on the same basis, has acquired title as the result of any irregularity of procedure in making a guardianship order, or that a financial guardian has acted outwith the scope of their authority [10].

## Contracts and other matters

In relation to the entering of contracts for the supply of goods and services, financial transactions and the like, the 2000 Act does not provide particularly clear guidance. In the case of powers of attorney, the attorney has power to enter such transactions as are contained in the deed until ended. As previously noted, the effect of making a guardianship order is that:-

> "The adult shall have no capacity to enter into any transaction in relation to any matter which is within the scope of the authority conferred on the guardian except in a case where he has been authorised by the guardian..." [11].

Section 67 then states that:-

"(4) The guardian shall be personally liable under any transaction entered into by him—

(a) without disclosing that he is acting as guardian of the adult; or

(b) which falls outwith the scope of his authority,

but where a guardian has acted as mentioned in paragraph (a) and is not otherwise in breach of any requirement of this Act relating to such guardians, he shall be entitled to be reimbursed from the estate of the adult in respect of any loss suffered by him in consequence of a claim made upon him personally by virtue of this subsection.

(5) Where a third party with whom the adult entered into a transaction was aware at the date of entering into the transaction that authority had been granted by the guardian under section 64(1)(e) [12], the transaction shall not be void only on the ground that the adult lacked capacity.

(6) A transaction for value between the guardian purporting to act as such and a third party acting in good faith shall not be invalid on the ground only that—

(a) the guardian acted outwith the scope of his authority; or

(b) the guardian failed to observe any requirement, whether substantive or procedural, imposed by or under this Act, or by the Sheriff or by the public guardian; or

(c) there was any irregularity whether substantive or procedural in the appointment of the guardian." [13].

The intended effect of these provisions appears to be one of protecting third parties from any irregularity in a transaction where they have acted properly in the process. Where the mere fact of a failure to disclose the capacity in which they act causes subs.(4) to apply, the guardian is entitled to offset any personal liability arising from the adult's estate.

Two further provisions should be kept in mind. The first is that s.24 (4) of the 2000 Act [14] is drafted in two parts, the first of which states that:-

> No liability shall be incurred by *any person* who acts in good faith in ignorance of—
>
> (a) the coming to an end of a power of attorney under subsection (1) or subsection (1A); or
>
> (b) the appointment of a guardian as mentioned in subsection (2)" [15].

There is no reported authority on how to interpret this provision, and the relevant explanatory note places emphasis on protection of dealings in heritable property, but this wording and the persons entitled to benefit is widely-drawn, and does not seem to exclude acts of an attorney or guardian.

The entitlement of a guardian, attorney, intervener or withdrawer to exclude liability for acts done in breach of any fiduciary duty or duty of care to an adult in good faith, and in accordance with the five principles [16] may also be relevant where a transaction is impugned.

The fundholder of an account created under an access to funds application is liable to the adult for any funds removed from the account where the fundholder was aware that a withdrawer's authority had been terminated or suspended by the public guardian [17].

## NOTES (CHAPTER 19)

1. 2000 Act, s.22A. See Chapter 7 above.
2. 2000 Act, s.23. See Chapter 7 above.
3. 2000 Act, s.22 (1) (c).
4. 2000 Act, s.24 (2). A power of attorney can also be terminated where the granter and attorney have been married to each other or in a civil partnership, where either ends.
5. See Chapters 13 & 14 above.
6. See Chapter 16 above.
7. 2000 Act, ss.56 (Intervention order) & 61 (Guardianship order).
8. 2000 Act, s.24 (4).
9. 2000 Act, s.77 (4).
10. 2000 Act, s.79.
11. 2000 Act, s.67 (1) 2000 Act, which is applied with modifications in relation to an Intervention Order (s.53 (14), 2000 Act). See also See *G's Guardians v Greater Glasgow Health Board 2021 GWD 40-533* at para.8.
12. A transaction authorised by the guardianship order. See Chapter 8 above.
13. 2000 Act, s.67 (4) – (5).
14. See FN 8 above.
15. Emphasis added. See Chapter 7 above.

16. 2000 Act, s.82. See Chapter 16 above.

17. 2000 Act, ss.29 & 33 (3). See Chapter 16 above. In such circumstances, the fundholder has a right of relief against the withdrawer.

# CHAPTER TWENTY

# DEPRIVATION OF AN ADULT'S LIBERTY

Where welfare powers have been created in relation to an adult with incapacity – whether by means of a power of attorney, guardianship order or intervention order, close consideration must be given is whether these bear to authorise the deprivation of liberty of the adult, and if so, whether it is lawful for such deprivation of liberty to occur. At present, this is a matter which is not expressly addressed by the 2000 Act.

The European Convention of Human Rights (EConHR) contains the following key provisions:-

> "Everyone has the right to liberty and security of person. No one shall be deprived of his liberty save in the following cases, and in accordance *with a procedure prescribed by law*..
>
> (e) the lawful detention.... of *persons of unsound mind*" [1].
>
> "Everyone who is deprived of his liberty by arrest or detention shall be entitled to take proceedings by which the *lawfulness of his detention* shall be decided speedily by a court..." [2].
>
> "Everyone has the right to respect for his home and his correspondence" ...There shall be no interference by a public authority with this right except such as is in accordance with the law and is necessary in a democratic society in the interests of...for the protection of health.... or for the protection of the rights and freedoms of others" [3].

What then is the position of any of these legally – effective documents which bear to authorise the detention or restriction of liberty of an adult who has lost capacity? It will be apparent that the process of granting a power of attorney is voluntary and independently certified to be the act of an adult with sufficient capacity [4]. On the other hand, its terms are not scrutinised by any court, and it appears unsupportable to argue that the registration of the power of attorney by the public guardian is the act of a "court".

Nevertheless, it is a situation likely to arise in the case of many adults who have become "incapable". It is commonplace for hospitals, care homes or nursing homes to impose restrictions on the movements of patients or residents, including having areas which are locked, which prevent their leaving of such premises.

What is open to question is whether – standing the terms of the EConHR quoted – such restrictions are lawful. The decisions of the European Court of Human Rights in *HL v United* Kingdom [5] and the UK Supreme Court in *Surrey CC v (P (Equality and Human Rights Commission Intervening)* [6] are particularly important.

In *Bournewood*, which concerned the circumstances of a young adult with incapacity who was living in a hospital, the Strasbourg Court made the observation that the concrete situation of the young man was that he was under continuous supervision and control, not free to leave the hospital, and therefore was deprived of his liberty in breach of art.5.1. Significantly, the Court stated that:-

> "The right to liberty in a democratic society is too important to be lost for the single reason that the individual had given themself up to be taken into detention, especially where there is no dispute that the applicant has been legally incapable of consenting to or disagreeing with the proposed action" [7].

This appears to establish that a deprivation of liberty can apply in many situations, but it appears to be no argument that even where this occurs with a benign intent and possibly in the adult's best interests, the breach of the art.5 right remains. Thus, in *Cheshire West,* the situations of two young adult women who were able to leave a foster home to attend education, and an older adult who, amongst other matters, required to wear restrictive clothing, were held also to breach the art.5 right.

Memorably, Lady Hale of Richmond declared that, notwithstanding the "homelike conditions" the individuals experienced:-

> "A gilded cage is still a cage" [8].

The question of whether a power of attorney authorising, for example, admission to a care home of the kind described – which impose these restrictions primarily for the safety of residents – can avoid breaching the Art.5 right of an adult who has become incapable.

Despite the decisions cited being nearly 25 years old in one case, Scotland still has no express legislation governing the deprivation or significant restriction of liberty of an incapable adult. The Scottish law commission has considered the issue in recent times, and has brought forward draft legislation, which has yet to be considered by the Scottish parliament [9].

In England and Wales, by contrast, the deprivation of liberty safeguards (DOLS) were introduced in 2005, in order to provide a process for authorising such actions [10]. In practice, the DOLS have proved unwieldy in practice, and will be replaced by the liberty protection safeguards (LPS) [11].

Other questions arise in relation to the inclusion of similar authority into a guardianship order or intervention order. In terms of the Human Rights Act 1998:-

> "It is unlawful for a public authority to act in a way which is incompatible with a Convention Right"

The 1998 Act also states that:

> "In this section "public authority" includes a court or tribunal" [12].

It may seem questionable in principle, therefore, whether the Sheriff can properly grant an order under the 2000 Act which authorises a breach of the Art.5 rights of an incapable adult. At present, the 2000 Act contains no express provision allowing the Court to grant such authorisation. Nevertheless, Sheriffs can and do grant orders in such terms, in one reported case Sheriff Baird concluded that the measure would be the "least restrictive option" for the adult [13].

Subsequently, the Sheriff Appeal Court stated in *K v Argyll and Bute Council* [14] that.

> "We recognise that s.64 does not contain an explicit power to detain but it seems to us that s.64(1)(a) and (b), subject to the application of the [s.1] principles, may usefully be deployed to address the very sad and unfortunate situation which has arisen here. In effect a detailed and bespoke care package has been created for the adult to address her specific needs. We are satisfied, given the factual matrix, that "a matter" or "all aspects" would cover dealing with the welfare issues of transitioning an adult from one form of care and accommodation (e.g. supported care at home) to another form of care and facility (e.g. care in secure premises), ensuring that the adult remains within the facility to address her needs, and to return her there should she leave." [15]

The current view of MWCS is that where, in the case of a power of attorney it cannot operate in conjunction with current good practice, to make decisions resulting in a deprivation of liberty, it is necessary to create a "clear and auditable process" for taking decisions on care arrangements for people to lack capacity. In such circumstances, the making of an application for welfare guardianship should be made, seeking specific authority for measures such as restraint, use of physical force, prevention of leaving a place and the use of intrusive surveillance [16].

What may be absent from the MWCS analysis is consideration of a potential lacuna where a guardianship order authorises measures which may prove excessive over time and in conflict with the five principles.

The default period of a guardianship order is three years [17], and a Court is not obliged to review the conditions in that time, unless triggered by action initiated on behalf of the adult. Where an adult remains "incapable" it is unlikely this option will be available. Overall, it may be doubted whether an element of arbitrariness is avoided by the current regime, and whether appropriate safeguards exist.

In Scotland, some reliance has been placed upon s.13ZA of the Social Work (Scotland) Act 1968, which provides that:

(1) Where—

(a) a local authority have decided under section 12A of this Act that an adult's needs call for the provision of a community care service; and

(b) it appears to the local authority that the adult is *incapable in relation to decisions about the service,*

the local authority may take *any steps* which they consider would help the adult to benefit from the service.

(2) Without prejudice to the generality of subsection (1) above, steps that may be taken by the local authority include *moving the adult to residential accommodation provided in pursuance of this Part.*

(3) The principles set out in subsection (2) to (4) of section 1 of the 2000 Act apply in relation to any steps taken under subsection (1) above as they apply to interventions in the affairs of an adult under or in pursuance of that Act" [18].

Again however, the 1968 Act makes no express provision which authorises the deprivation or restriction of the liberty of an adult who, in order to fall within the test provided by the 2000 Act, must satisfy a further test of "incapacity" at the time of being moved [19].

A further issue, if presently more remote, is how such restrictions can be imposed compatibly with the CRPD, and particularly art.14 which states that:-

> "States Parties shall ensure that persons with disabilities, on an equal basis with others:-
>
> (a) enjoy the right to liberty and security of person
>
> (b) are not deprived of their liberty unlawfully or arbitrarily, and that any deprivation of liberty is in conformity with the law, and that the existence of a disability shall in no case justify a deprivation of liberty".

It is beyond the scope of this work to engage in a detailed analysis of whether the scheme of the 2000 Act is currently compliant with the EConHR and/or the CRPD. Nevertheless, the question raised by the English Court of Protection when it refused to register a Scottish Guardianship Order under the Mental Capacity Act 2005 [20] is eloquent of the kind of uncertainty created by the absence of a legislative framework for authorising a deprivation of liberty.

The Scottish government consulted on implementation of the CRPD and published *Recommendations for a new human rights framework to improve people's lives* in December 2018, which contains proposals for legislation which would embrace all forms of human rights. Following the establishments of a national taskforce for human rights leadership, which published a report in 2021 [21], the Scottish government subsequently announced its intention to incorporate the CRPD into a Human Rights bill.

As is considered in more detail in Chapter 24, a major review of the legislation in this field has been completed., and at the time of writing, the Scottish Government is consulting on how this critical matter can be resolved in legislation. Suffice to say at this stage that a regime in Scotland authorising deprivation of liberty of an incapable adult which is compliant with the EConHR is still some way distant.

Consequently, it is submitted that the legal mechanism for imposing a deprivation of liberty upon an adult with incapacity remains unsatisfactory. The founding SLC Report has remains unimplemented, and the uncertainty first established in *Bournewood* some 20 years ago, remains signally unresolved. The continuation of this situation is subject to severe recent criticism [22], and leaves the Scottish Government at risk of having its hand forced through litigation during the intervening time.

## NOTES (CHAPTER 20)

1. EConHR, art.5.1 (Emphasis added).

2. EConHR, art.5.4 (Emphasis added).

3. EConHR, art.8.1 & 2

4. See Chapter 5 above.

5. [2005] 40 EHRR 3 (Usually referred to as "*Bournewood*").

6. [2014] AC 896 (Usually referred to as "*Cheshire West*").

7. At paras. 89 – 90.

8. At para.46. See also *Re D (A Child) [2017] EWCA 1695* (described as "the teenage *Bournewood*").

9. *Report on Adults with Incapacity* (SLC Report No.240 (2014)).

10. Mental Capacity Act 2005, Schedule A1.

11. Mental Capacity (Amendment) Act 2019, s.1 (4). The date for implementation of the LPS has been deferred more than once from their enactment, and this is not expected to occur before than January 2025 at the earliest.

12. Human Rights Act 1998, s.6(1) and (3) (a).

13. *Muldoon Applicant 2005 SLT (Sh.Ct.) 52* at para.58K. Followed in *M Applicant* 2009 SLT (Sh.Ct.) 185.

14. *2*021 SLT (SAC) 29.

15. At para.28. See also *Scottish Borders Council v AB, 2020 S.L.T. (Sh Ct) 41.*

16. *Common concerns with powers of attorney* (MWCS) (April 2021), pp.12 & 13.

17. See Chapter 9 above.

18. Inserted by the Adult Support and Protection (Scotland) Act 2007, s.64 (Emphases added). Powers under s.13ZA require to be exercised in accordance with the five principles (s.13ZA (3)). A local authority cannot exercise the s.13ZA power where the adult has a welfare guardian or welfare attorney with powers relating to the proposed steps has been appointed, or where an intervention order has been granted relating to the proposed steps. The making of an application for an intervention order or guardianship order relating to the proposed steps also prevents use of this power (1968 Act, s.13ZA (4)).

19. See Chapter 5 above.

20. *Aberdeenshire Council v SF (No.2) [2024] EWCOP* 10. See also Chapter 2 above.

21. https://www.gov.scot/publications/national-taskforce-human-rights-leadership-report/.

22. See, for example, Adrian Ward, *Scotland: A Human Rights Blackspot (Parts 1-3)* 2024 SLT (News) 59, 65 & 71.

# CHAPTER TWENTY-ONE

# NEGOTIATING A CARE PACKAGE

In many cases, an adult with incapacity will both require and be entitled to some form of care support, whether or not they can continue to live in the community. This issue will impact upon those acting under powers of attorney, financial and welfare guardianship and possibly intervention orders.

Such entitlements most likely stem from a community care assessment made by the local authority for the area in which the adult resides. This process may be initiated by the local authority itself, or in response to a request [1].

The assessment is required to address the individual's needs for "community care services" [2]. These are services which the local authority has a duty or power to provide under Part 2 of the 1968 Act. This is broadly expressed as meaning:-

> "arrangements ...to provide or secure the provision of such facilities (including the provision or arranging for the provision of residential and other establishments) as they may consider suitable or adequate" [3].

Part of that process is stated to include:-

> "insofar as is reasonable and practicable to do so... of the views of the person whose needs are being assessed... (provided that there is a wish, or as the case may be, a capacity, to express a view, whether the needs of the person being assessed call for the provision of any such services" [4].

In response, the local authority must state how it proposes to meet these needs. The House of Lords clarified in *Robertson v Fife Council* [5] that the individual's needs for care comes first and the requirement to pay what can be afforded and any charges to be applied comes at a later stage.

In this event, the next stage is for the individual to choose one of the statutory options for self – directed support [6]. Prior to deciding whether an individual requires nursing care, the local authority requires to consult a medical practitioner [7].

The scheme for self-directed support is premised upon payments being made to the "supported person" by selection from a number of options. In the event that the local authority consider that the "supported person" is ineligible to receive direct payments, the reasons for so deciding must be notified, and certain options will not be available as a result [8].

Under the 2013 Act, where needs have been identified, the local authority must offer 1 of 4 Options

Option 1 Direct payment to the "supported person"

Option 2 The "supported person" decides what support is needed, but that support is arranged and paid for by the local authority

Option 3 The local authority decides what support is required and arranges and pays for it.

Option 4 Combination of options 1,2,3 [9].

Where support is to be provided by someone other than the local authority, the amount payable to the "supported person" is the "relevant amount", which represents the local authority's "reasonable estimate" of the cost of securing that support [10].

The local authority must take "reasonable steps" to provide support in selecting an option where no welfare attorney, welfare guardian or intervener with welfare powers is available to an adult. This obtains where benefit would accrue to a "supported person" as a result of "mental disorder" [11], or where this would assist communication of decisions as a result of difficulties arising from physical disabilities [12].

## Assessing the care budget

There is no prescribed method in statute for determining what an adult's care budget should be. As a result, local authorities have adopted several methods of assessing the figure, and it is the duty of the local authority to inform the adult of the "relevant amount" for each of the options for SDS which the adult is being given the opportunity to choose, and the period for which it is available. Where the adult does not make such a choice, option 3 is imposed as a default option [13].

The two systems of assessment of needs of the adult and the care budget thereby generated which are employed generally are:-

A: Resource Allocation System (RAS)

This is the most frequently applied methodology and essentially proceeds by means of joint completion of a self-evaluation questionnaire, which results in a scoring which then awards funds on a sliding scale according to the number of points gained.

B: Equivalence Model

This process leads to the determination of the cost of services to be provided to an adult and the equivalent Budget to be awarded. This allows the support to be varied within the cost envelope provided.

Either method will produce a care budget to be expended in accordance with one of Options 1 – 4.

## Cost of service provided

In the provision of "community care services" a local authority is entitled to recover:-

> "such charge (if any) for it as they consider reasonable" [14].

However, where the recipient can satisfy the local authority that their:-

> "means are insufficient for it to be reasonably practicable ...to pay for the service the amount [they] would be obliged to pay for it, the authority shall not require him to pay more for it than appears to them that it is practicable for them to pay" [15].

The practical effect is that in the provision of "community care services" generally, local authorities will apply a charging scheme which means tests the ability of the recipient to pay for some or all of the care budget initially assessed, and to deduct a sum from the figure generated by the assessment of the adult's needs.

The operation of this process has received recent scrutiny up to the level of the UKSC in *McCue's Guardian v Glasgow City Council* [16]. Here, the mother and guardian of a young incapable adult, raised a petition for judicial review of the local authority's calculation of a contribution to the "community care services" being provided to her son.

The local authority operated a charging policy under which a liability to make contributions was triggered by exceeding a "minimum income threshold" calculated by reference to guidance issued by COSLA [17] and rates set by the DWP. Even after disregarding the DLA paid to him, the young adult's income exceeded the threshold.

The question then became to what extent, his liability to contribute could be reduced by taking into account "disability related expenditure", the correct level of which was disputed. In essence, the local authority considered that the purpose of the adult's care plan was such that the disputed sums were discretionary choices and therefore, not taken into account.

The UKSC observed that the local authority which has the function of forming a judgment whether the individual's means are insufficient to the extent that it is not 'practicable' for the individual to pay for the services provided. The onus was on the individual to satisfy the local. authority of this. It further noted that the term "disability related expenditure" did not have any statutory basis, and the relevant question, having regard to subsec (1A), was whether the council was satisfied that Mr McCue, by his expenditure on the various items in dispute, had shown that his means were insufficient for it to be reasonably practicable for him to pay for the community care services provided to him by the council, such that it was not 'practicable' for him to pay a charge calculated without deduction of those items. [18].

Further, expenditure could be related to disability in the relevant sense if it is used to meet other needs of the individual arising by reason of his disability, so long as those needs are so pressing that the relevant local authority assesses (or should assess) that expenditure to meet them has the effect that, to that extent, the individual's means are reduced below what it would otherwise be practicable for him to pay as a charge for the services provided by the authority. Accordingly, the deductions made by the Council were held to have been correctly made in terms of its relevant policies [19].

As is outlined elsewhere in this Chapter, making a successful challenge to the assessment of the charges for Community Care services imposed in an individual case is an onerous task. The Courts are wary of reviewing a specific outcome arising from an exercise of the Local Authority's discretion in accordance with its own policies. It also appears that making a successful challenge of a policy overall on grounds such as breach of the Equality Act 2010 may prove equally demanding. A challenge to the policies of the local authority made in *McCue v Glasgow CC* which was based upon the Equality Act 2010 was rejected by the UKSC [19].

One issue requiring to be kept in mind arises from the Self – Directed Support (Direct Payments) (Scotland) Regulations 2014, which provides that:-

> "a family member may not provide support to which a direct payment relates if—
>
> "....the family member is a guardian, continuing attorney or welfare attorney with power to make decisions as regards the support to be provided through the direct payment." [20].

Challenging the determination

Inevitably, there will be tension between what an adult or their representatives consider is necessary to meet their needs and the assessments made by the local authority. The fact that resources available necessarily are finite and under considerable pressure for the foreseeable future cannot be discounted, albeit a power need not be exercised, but a duty must be discharged [21].

Normally, some form of internal review mechanism will be operated by a local authority, allowing the initial outcome to be reconsidered at a more senior level of management. If unsuccessful there, the process for further challenge can become complicated.

In principle, a decision made in exercise of a statutory jurisdiction is capable of being subjected to judicial review on the normal *Wednesbury* grounds. In short, that will not involve a Court in determining whether the care budget assessed was one which it would have created, but rather whether an error of law can be identified in the process. Nevertheless, the Courts do not appear to exclude making a challenge to a care budget where the application of the system has been flawed [22].

Judicial review normally is open only once available means of challenge of a decision have been exhausted. A judicial review will normally require to be commenced within 3 months of the disputed decision, albeit the

Court has a discretion to allow petitions lodged beyond that time [23]. Even if that hurdle can be surmounted and permission to proceed obtained [24], the matter potentially can be rendered academic by the local authority conducting a further assessment of the adult, which effectively resets the entire process.

The scope of discretion available to the local authority in operating the SDS system was outlined in *Q v Glasgow CC*. There, Lord Boyd of Duncansby stated in the Outer House that it was for the person challenging the level of payment calculated to show that it was not a reasonable estimate of the cost of securing the care provision; it was not for the local authority to demonstrate the tools used to reach that estimate [25].

This case also illustrates the extent of the discretion afforded to a local authority in reaching decisions under the 2013 Act. The issue concerned an 87 year-old woman with vascular dementia, who initially returned to live at home with a 24-hour care package. She was then assessed by GCC as requiring nursing home care. In the course this decision being challenged – the difference in the annual care budget amounting to £600. When the decision of the Lord Ordinary was appealed, the Inner House held that:-

(a) in discharging the duty under s.12A of the 1968 Act, GCC was required to make an assessment of needs and it had to decide whether the needs called for the provision of community care services and it was implicit therein to decide the nature and extent of care services called for;

(b) the fact that the relevant person's combination of impairments put her at particular risk of falling and the opinions expressed in the expert reports relied upon by the adult's family might have provided support for the proposition that her needs called for one-to-one care, it did not follow that GCC's assessment which concluded that those needs called for a less intensive degree of care was irrational or perverse;

(c) that GCC's estimate of cost did not depend on an application of the resource allocation tool where the exercise had been rejected in favour of a simple estimate of the cost of services, GCC was entitled to conclude that the relevant person's needs were not so different from other elderly persons at risk from falls, that while 24-hour care was called for, that could be provided in a care home without one to one supervision and attention

(d) having so concluded, GCC had arrived at what it considered to be a reasonable estimate of the cost of securing the relevant services for the subject having regard to the level of the cost charged by nursing homes within its local authority area for providing equivalent services which it was fully entitled to do [26].

It is important to appreciate also that the Courts will not scrutinise a care plan as if as if it was a conveyancing document. In one case in England, it was stated that these should be construed in a practical way against the factual background in which they are written with the aim of seeking to discover the substance of their true meaning [27].

It can reasonably be inferred therefore, that in most cases, it will not be the responsibility of a local authority to demonstrate that a decision on a care budget is reasonable, but that the burden of demonstrating a perverse or unreasonable outcome will rest with an adult or their representatives. As noted, it is important to bear in mind that in the time required to bring a challenge before the Courts, the needs of the adult may have been re-assessed rendering the impugned decision academic.

The effect of a complaints procedure

Even if an argument challenging the assessment of a care package can be stated, further issues require to be addressed. Prior to April 2017, local authorities were required by statute to provide a further level of appeal under a complaints procedure [28]. In the past, the Courts have emphasised the need for a local authority to have a complaints procedure in relation to determinations on Self – directed support [29], and also that consideration should be given to making a user-friendly guide to the system for determining care budgets [30]

The previous complaints arrangements were replaced by amendments to the Scottish Public Services Ombudsman Act 2002 which qualified the prohibition of the SPSO questioning:-

> "the merits of a decision taken without maladministration by… [a] local authority in the exercise of a discretion vested in that authority"

where a matter concerned:-

> "the merits of a decision taken by [a local authority] in pursuance of a social work function in consequence of the exercise of the professional judgement of the social worker…discharging the function" [31].

However, the SPSO also is prohibited from investigating a matter where a person has:-

> "a remedy by way of proceedings in any court of law, unless the Ombudsman is satisfied that, in the particular circumstances, it is not reasonable to have expected the person aggrieved to resort or have resorted to this right or remedy" [32]

In *McCue's Guardian v Glasgow City Council* [33], the Inner House determined that judicial review fell within the definition of "a remedy by way of proceedings" [34]. The Court concluded that where proceedings for judicial review are presented, the jurisdiction of the SPSO on the same matters would be ousted.

The Court determined that where a complainer had elected not to pursue a judicial review, it remained open to the SPSO to decide whether to accept the complaint, subject to taking a view on whether an obvious legality point or question of law requiring to be determined by a Court. The final decision on whether a matter was more appropriate for the SPSO remained open to the Court which could still dismiss a petition as not amenable to the supervisory jurisdiction [35].

It is submitted that while reference to the SPSO is not an essential prerequisite to initiating judicial review proceedings, scope exists for significant doubt regarding what is the best course of challenge to an adverse SDS outcome. If a reference to SPSO is rejected, little time may remain to meet the three-month time limit for lodging a petition. On the other hand, if a Judicial review petition is lodged timeously but then refused for some reason, considerable time is likely to have elapsed before SPSO completes its consideration of the disputed assessment.

Finally, it should be kept in mind that Lord Boyd of Duncansby observed in *Q v Glasgow CC* that where an error of law was found in a decision, it was for the local authority to remake the decision correctly, possibly under the Court's guidance, but not for the Court to do so [36]. Accordingly, the practical effect of a matter returning to a local authority to reconsider, even where a judicial review has succeeded, may be a significant time in arriving.

It can be seen, therefore, that challenging an adverse decision on a care package is potentially complex. Arguably, the current situation mandates early involvement in the assessment and review process in order that factual errors or invalid methodologies are addressed before resort to the Courts or SPSO actually arises. It may also be more practicable to wait to see whether a future assessment of whether the effect of an inadequate assessment is more apparent, and more open to challenge.

## NOTES (CHAPTER 21)

1. Social Work (Scotland) Act 1968, s.12A.

2. 1968 Act, s.12 (1) & (8)).

3. 1968 Act, s.12 (1).

4. 1968 Act, s.12A (b) (ii), as amended by the Community Care and Health (Scotland) Act 2002, s.8).

5. 2002 SC (HL) 145, at para.53.

6. Self Directed Support (Scotland) Act 2013, s.5 (2).

7. 1968 Act, s.12A (2).

8. 2013 Act, s.5(3). See Self – Directed Support (Direct Payments) (Scotland) Regulations 2014 (SSI 2014/25).

9. 2013 Act, s.4 (1).

10. 2013 Act, s.4.

11. See 2003 Act, s.328.

12. 2013 Act, s.6. See also 1968 Act, s12A (4)).

13. 2013 Act, s.5 (4) & (5).

14. 1968 Act, s.87 (1).

15. 1968 Act, s.87 (1A). It should be noted that a local authority cannot charge for "social care" provided by them as is defined by the Community Care and Health (Scotland) Act 2002 (See *Boath v Perth and Kinross Council* 2009 SLT 627).

16. 2023 SC (UKSC) 69. (Previously reported at 2021 SC 41 (IH) and 2019 SC 107 (OH)).

17. See National *Strategy and Guidance: Charges applying to social care support for people at home 2022/2023 (COSLA, 2022)*, section 6.

18. Per Lord Sales JSC at paras.43, 44 & 46.

19. At paras.50–52.

20. Regulations, regn.9 (2).

21. *Q v Glasgow CC 2016* CSOH 137, at para.17.

22. At para.54. As noted above and elsewhere in this Chapter, the practicality of finding an issue in which the Courts will Intervene is a formidable challenge. In *BB v Glasgow City Council [2024] CSOH 44*, the application of a Taper of [allowable free income] in imposing Social Care Charges under s.87 1968 Act was challenged under the Equality Act 2010 as having a discriminatory effect. GCC acknowledged that it had failed to carry out an adequate equality impact assessment in compliance with the PSED and while Lord Boyd of Duncansby granted a Declarator to that effect, he declined to reduce the Policy itself (At paras. 57–59). (c.f. *McHattie v South Ayrshire Council [2020] SLT 399*). Court of Session Act 1988, s.27A, as inserted by the Courts Reform (Scotland) Act 2014, s.89.

23. See Court of Session Act 1988, ss.27A, as inserted by the Courts Reform (Scotland) Act 2014, s.89.

24. Court of Session Act 1988 ss.27 B-D, as inserted by the Courts Reform (Scotland) Act 1988, s.89.

25 2018 SLT 151, at paras.20, 22 & 30. In the Outer House, Lord Boyd of Duncansby had observed that was it is not for the Court to take a decision which Parliament had empowered to the local

authority, and that the Court will acknowledge the finite resources available to a local authority (2016 CSOH 137, para.17. See also *R (G) v Barnet LBC* [2004] AC 208, para.14).

26. *McCue v Glasgow CC* 2014 SLT 891 at para.51 and *Smart's Guardian v Fife Council* 2016 SLT 384.

27. *R (McDonald) v Kensington and Chelsea RLBC [2011] UKSC 33*, where a major issue involved was a comparison of "one to one care" against "24 hours care". This approach was endorsed by the Outer House in *Q v Glasgow CC* (at para.17).

28. 1968 Act, s.5B (now repealed).

29. *Smart's Guardian v Fife Council* 2016 SLT 384, at para.18.

30. *Q v Glasgow City Council* 2018 SLT 151, at para.30.

31.Scottish Public Services Ombudsman Act 2002, s.7 (1) & (2C)-(2E).

32. 2002 Act, s.7 (8).

33. 2020 SLT 963.

34. At para.44.

35. At para.45. The Court observed that the effect of the legislation, in our view, is that it was open to the SPSO to consider in a complaint the merits of any decision made in respect of the care provision for Andrew, or the management of it, notwithstanding that the decision involved a degree of professional judgment. As one example, a decision in general terms, whether the appropriate sums for DRE had been deducted from the section 87(1A) charge, could come within the jurisdiction of the SPSO, as also an alleged failure to respond to a complaint (At para.56).

36. At para.16.

# CHAPTER TWENTY-TWO

# DEALING WITH EMERGENCIES

It is important that anyone who acts under a power of attorney, guardianship or intervention order is aware of other statutory powers which they may exercise or which may be exercised in relation to an adult with incapacity. It is possible that a significant deterioration of the adult's physical and/or mental health may occur, or it becomes apparent that the adult is at imminent risk of coming to some kind of harm.

Where a welfare guardian is in place, specific powers can be applied where the adult refuses to comply with directions of the welfare guardian [1], but this will not necessarily achieve an early result. It may also be possible to seek directions from the Sheriff in terms of s.3 the 2000 Act, but the efficacy of such measures in removing potential harm to an adult cannot be assumed [2]. Accordingly, resort to powers under the Adult Support and Protection (Scotland) Act 2007 or the Mental Health (Care and Treatment) (Scotland) Act 2003 may be necessary.

The 2007 Act focuses on the situation of an "adult at risk". This is defined as meaning an adult who:

(a) "[is] unable to safeguard their own well-being, property, rights or other interests

(b) [is] at risk of harm, and

(c) because they are affected by disability, mental disorder, illness or physical or mental infirmity, are more vulnerable to being harmed than adults who are not so affected." [3].

An adult is "at risk of harm" where:-

> "(a) another person's conduct is causing (or is likely to cause) the adult to be harmed, or;
>
> ...
>
> (c) the adult is engaging (or is likely to engage) in conduct which causes (or is likely to cause) self-harm" [4].

"Harm" can arise in a number of situations, but includes physical harm and conduct which causes self – harm and also:-

> "...conduct which causes psychological harm (for example: by causing fear, alarm or distress)... unlawful conduct which appropriates or adversely affects property, rights or interests (for example: theft, fraud, embezzlement or extortion)" [5].

Removal orders

In a situation of emergency, an adult can become subject to a removal order, for which a council [6] requires to make an application to the Sheriff. The Sheriff can grant a removal order only where satisfied that the adult concerned is "adult at risk" who is likely to be "seriously harmed" if not moved to another place, and also that the place to which the adult is to be moved is both available and suitable [7].

A council officer is entitled to enter any place in order to move an adult at risk from the place in pursuance of a removal order [8]. Provision is made for the Sheriff to vary or recall a removal order if satisfied that the variation or recall is justified by a change in the facts or circumstances in respect of which the order was granted or, as the case may be, last varied [9]. The council is required to take "reasonable steps" to prevent any property owned or controlled by an adult moved in pursuance of a removal order from being lost or damaged [10].

A similar form of removal order can be obtained under the Mental Health (Care and Treatment) (Scotland) Act 2003 where an adult satisfies the criterion of having a "mental disorder" under that legislation [11].

It will be appreciated that any resort to such powers potentially is draconian and distressing for an adult who may be summarily moved from their residence or lose control of some of their property. It is important to ensure that averments can be made in support of a removal order which will establish the necessity for such a step to be taken, and its conformity with the principles of the 2007 [12] Act In situations of sufficient risk however, a removal order may be an effective protective alternative where an intervention order or authority to intromit need too much time to obtain.

<u>Banning orders</u>

The 2007 Act provides a more limited form of protection to vulnerable adults in the form of a banning order. Such an order is:-

> "an order granted by the sheriff which bans the subject of the order from being in a specified place." [13].

A wider range of measures can be authorised in a banning order, which include:-

> "(a) [banning] the subject from being in a specified area in the vicinity of the specified place,
>
> (b) [authorising] the summary ejection of the subject from the specified place and the specified area,
>
> (c) [prohibiting] the subject from moving any specified thing from the specified place..." [14].

An application for a banning order may be made only by or on behalf of [15]—

> "(a) an adult whose well-being or property would be safeguarded by the order;
>
> (b) any other person who is entitled to occupy the place concerned, or
>
> (c) …the council" [16].

The criteria for granting a banning order require the Sheriff to be satisfied that:-

> "(a) that an adult at risk is being, or is likely to be, seriously harmed by another person,
>
> (b) that the adult at risk's well-being or property would be better safeguarded by banning that other person from a place occupied by the adult than it would be by moving the adult from that place, and
>
> (c) that either—
>
> (i) the adult at risk is entitled, or permitted by a third party, or
>
> (ii) neither the adult at risk nor the subject is entitled, or permitted by a third party,
>
> to occupy the place from which the subject is to be banned" [17].

Notification of making of the banning order requires to be given to:-

> (a) "the adult whose well-being or property is safeguarded by the order, and
>
> (b) any other person with an interest in that adult's well-being or property as the sheriff may specify." [18].

It will be apparent that, in some circumstances, an adult with incapacity will satisfy the definition of an "adult at risk" who might best be protected by the obtaining of a banning order. One clear advantage is that a banning order does not entail the removal of an adult from the place where they are resident, whereas a removal order has that effect. Moreover, the subject of a banning order potentially risks arrest for breaching its terms [19].

The requirement of notifying the adult potentially may carry the risk of a different form of harm or distress to the adult. It would seem possible for this step to be elided by applying the principles set out in ss.1 & 2 of the 2007 Act. This may explain why a failure to comply with the provision does not invalidate the terms of the banning order [20].

As with removal orders, provision exists for the variation or recall of a banning order [21].

## NOTES (CHAPTER 22)

1. See Chapter 11 above.

2. See Chapter 4 above.

3. 2007 Act, s.3 (1). The statutory definition is considered in *North Lanarkshire Council v BM & NM 2023 SCLR 1.*

4. 2007 Act, s.3 (2).

5. 2007 Act, s.53.

6. In s.53 (1) of the 2007 Act, the term "council" is defined as being one which is established under the Local Government Etc. (Scotland) Act 1994, which in practice, is a local authority. The provisions of the 2007 Act are applied for this purpose to "the area for which the person is for the time being in", presumably to avoid consideration of issues of habitual or actual residence obstructing their use.

7. 2007 Act, s.14 (1). The relevant procedural provisions are set out in the SAR 1999, r.3.35.1 – 9. (A removal order can also require a "specified person" to have contact with the adult concerned (2007 Act, s.14 (2) & (3)).

8. 2007 Act, s.16.

9. 2007 Act, s17.

10. 2007 Act, s.18.

11. 2003 Act, ss.292–298 & 328. See Chapter 2 in relation to the meaning assigned to "mental disorder".

12. It should be noted that a set of principles are set out in ss.1 & 2 of the 2007 Act governing the making of interventions relating to an

adult generally, which are broadly similar to those set out in s.1 of the 2000 Act.

13. 2007 Act, s.19 (1).

14. 2007 Act, s.19 (2) (a) – (c).

15. 2007 Act, s.22 (1). It is submitted that this wording is apt to include persons acting under a power of attorney, guardianship order or intervention order. The wording of "any person having an interest in the property and welfare of the adult" applied in the 2000 Act has not been adopted here (c.f. s.26 (2)).

16. 2007 Act, s.22 (1). The "council" is required to seek a banning order in circumstances where the criteria for granting a banning order are satisfied, but no one else is likely to make such an application (s.22 (2)). The provisions governing an application for a banning order are set out in SAR r.3.35.3.

17. 2000 Act, s.20. How these criteria can apply in practice was considered in *North Lanarkshire Council v BM & NM* (See paras. 8 & 9 and 37 – 45). It is also possible for the Sheriff to impose a temporary banning order (s.21).

18. 2007 Act, s.26 (2).

19. 2007 Act, ss.25, 28 – 34 (s.30 is repealed).

20. 2007 Act, s.26 (4).

21. 2007 Act, s.24.

# CHAPTER TWENTY-THREE

# MEDICAL TREATMENT

Where an adult loses the capacity to give consent to medical treatment, particularly serious issues can arise in relation to the proper authorisation of any proposed procedures or treatments. "Medical treatment" as defined by the 2000 Act is:-

> "any procedure or treatment designed to safeguard or promote physical or mental health" [1].

Potentially, this can range from a general examination through routine dentistry to major and potentially life – saving surgical procedures. It is beyond the scope of this work to examine closely the law and ethics underlying the critical principle of a patient providing an informed consent to any procedure. For present purposes, what will be considered are the provisions made where the capacity of an adult to give such consent is absent.

One matter where the principles applying under the 2000 Act have particular significance are previous statements by the adult – whether written or verbal – expressing a desire not to undergo a procedure, but which a doctor considers to be clinically appropriate nonetheless. Conversely, during the coronavirus epidemic, considerable controversy attended the placing of do not resuscitate (DNR) or do not attempt CPR (DNCPR) notices in the medical notes of an incapable adult. This is a particularly acute matter where such notices were lodged without the knowledge of the adult's relatives or else their welfare attorney or welfare guardian who stand in their place under the order appointing them [2].

Provisions for the giving of "medical treatment" to an adult with incapacity are set out in the 2000 Act, ss.47 – 52. The procedure provides authorisation to do:-

> "what is reasonable in the circumstances, in relation to the medical treatment in question, to safeguard or promote the physical or mental health of the adult"

where an adult is certified to be "incapable in relation to a decision about the "medical treatment" in question [3].

A range of medical practitioners [4], which may include the adult's GP, who has issued the certificate, will obtain:

> "during the period specified in the certificate, authority to do what is reasonable in the circumstances, in relation to the medical treatment in question, to safeguard or promote the physical or mental health of the adult" [5].

Certain forms of medical treatment can only be given in furtherance of a s.47 certificate where authorised by the Court of Session or by a practitioner appointed by the MWCS [6].

In order to issue a s.47 certificate, the granter must be of the opinion that:

> "The adult is incapable in relation to a decision about the medical treatment in question and make a statement to that effect, which specifies the period during which such authority shall subsist" [7]

The certificate issued requires to state how long the incapacity is "likely to continue" and should not normally endure beyond one year [8]. It is possible for the period of the authorisation to be extended to three years in prescribed circumstances [9]. This includes severe and profound learning disability which is "unlikely to improve", dementia or a severe neurological disorder [10].

In the event of a change in the adult's condition or circumstances, the granter of the certificate may revoke the original and may issue a fresh certificate under the same provisions [11].

A s.47 certificate does not authorise:-

(a) the use of force or detention, unless it is immediately necessary and only for so long as is necessary in the circumstances;

(b) action which would be inconsistent with any decision by a competent court;

(c) placing an adult in a hospital for the treatment of mental disorder against his will [12].

Authority to give treatment under a s.47 certificate is suspended while it is subject to proceedings in any court which have not been determined, or where provision of the treatment is the subject of an interdict [13].

The authority of the granter of a s.47 certificate also is suspended where the granter is aware of an application having been made for a guardianship order or intervention order which is undetermined [14]. Medical treatment may still be given in this instance, where it is authorised by any other enactment or rule of law for the preservation of the life of the adult or the prevention of serious deterioration in his medical condition. This exception cannot be applied where the proposed treatment is the subject of an interdict [15].

Suspension of s.47 authority

The appointment of a welfare attorney, welfare guardian or the granting of authority under an intervention order concerning medical treatment in relation to an incapable adult, also has the effect of suspending the authority of the granter of a s.47 certificate where:-

(i) the granter is aware of the appointment and

(ii) has failed to obtain the consent of the welfare attorney, welfare guardian or intervener to any medical treatment, where it is reasonable and practicable to do so [16].

Even so, a welfare guardian cannot:-

(a) place the adult in a hospital for the treatment of mental disorder against [their] will; . . .

(b) consent on behalf of the adult to any form of treatment in relation to which the authority conferred by section 47(2) does not apply by virtue of regulations made under section 48(2) [17].

A complex set of provisions addresses circumstances where the granter of a s.47 certificate disagrees with a welfare attorney, welfare guardian or intervener, which can result in authority to give medical treatment being granted by a "nominated practitioner" appointed by the MWCS, or by the Court of Session. [18]. For the purposes of s.50, a guardian or welfare attorney includes persons appointed or granted equivalent powers under the law of countries other than Scotland [19].

Aside from the procedure for making appeals to the Court of Session made by s.50:-

> "Any decision taken for the purposes of Part 5,... as to the medical treatment of the adult may be appealed by any person having an interest in the personal welfare of the adult to the sheriff and thence, with the leave of the sheriff, to the Court of Session" [20].

Other mental health matters

It is important to have an appreciation of the interrelationship of other statutory provisions with the 2000 Act. In the 2003 Act, "learning disability" is included in the definition of "mental disorder" in respect of which the various powers specified in that legislation may be exercised [21]. Conversely, in the 2000 Act, "incapacity" in defined in a more wide-sense than "mental disorder", embracing matters such as physical inability to communicate or the consequences of a stroke [22].

Two possible examples are circumstances where a patient who is detained in hospital under the 2003 Act as a result of their "mental disorder", but additionally requires the appointment of a financial and/or welfare guardian or intervener. Conversely, the condition of an adult who satisfies the definition of "incapacity" in the 2000 Act, may become subject to measures authorised under the 2003 Act, which could include, for example, detention in a hospital or becoming subject to a community – based compulsory treatment order, both of which can authorise the giving of "medical treatment" as defined under the 2003 Act [23].

It is possible to envisage circumstances in which an adult finds themselves subject to both pieces of legislation simultaneously. It is important, therefore, to keep in mind that different tests may apply under the 2000 and 2003 Acts.

## NOTES (CHAPTER 23)

1. 2000 Act, s.47 (4).

2. See *Covid – 19 FAQs for Practitioners* MWCS (2021), para.9.2.

3. 2000 Act, s.47 (1) (a) & (2).

4. See 2000 Act, s.47 (1A) & (11).

5. 2000 Act, s.47 (2).

6. 2000 Act, s.48. (See Adults with Incapacity (Specified Medical Treatments) (Scotland) Regulations 2002 for the forms of treatment subject to s.48).

7. 2000 Act, s.47 (5). (For the form of the certificate, see the Adults with Incapacity (Medical Treatment Certificates) (Scotland) Regulations 2007. See also the Adults with Incapacity (Requirements for Signing Medical Treatment Certificates) (Scotland) Regulations 2007).

8. 2000 Act, s.47 (5) (b) (i).

9. See Adults with Incapacity (Conditions and Circumstances Applicable to Three Year Medical Certificates) (Scotland) Regulations 2007.

10. 2007 Regulations, regn.2. The same grounds apply where an extension of the certificate is under consideration (Regn.3).

11. 2000 Act, s.47 (6).

12. 2000 Act, s.47 (7). This applies whether or not a patient has a "mental disorder".

13. 2000 Act, s.47 (9) & (10).

14. 2000 Act, s. 49 (1). In the unreported case of *CJR v JMR*, Kirkcaldy Sheriff Court, 27th February 2013, Sheriff Thornton granted a welfare guardianship order, authorising the welfare guardian to "arrange and, where necessary, consent or withhold consent to any medical treatment for the adult on the basis that leaving provision of medical treatment for the adult concerned to a series of s.47 certificates would be ad hoc and subject to challenge (At para.18).

15. 2000 Act, s.49 (2) & (3).

16. 2000 Act, s.50 (1) & (2).

17. 2000 Act, s.64 (2).

18. 2000 Act, s.50 (3) – (9).

19. 2000 Act, s.50 (10).

20. 2000 Act, s.52. Such an appeal initially would be made as a summary application (See SAR, r.3.16.7). See Chapter 15 above.

21. Mental Health (Care and Treatment) (Scotland) Act 2003, s.328.

22. 2000 Act, s.1 (6).

23. See 2003 Act, s.328, which expressly links the "medical treatment" which it authorises solely as a treatment for "mental disorder".

# CHAPTER TWENTY-FOUR

# THINGS TO COME – TOWARDS A 2030 ACT?

At the time of writing, the law relating to adults with incapacity is slated for extensive review and changes of potentially significant impact. How such changes may materialise ultimately fell to the *Review of mental health law in Scotland* under the chairmanship of John Scott QC [1].

The *Review* issued its final report in September 2022, and it will be understood that the remit of the *Review* goes significantly beyond the terms of 2000 Act, which has operated for over 20 years. In the long awaited Response by the Scottish Government [2] it is apparent the process of passing what is likely to be lengthy legislation may well extend through the term of the next Scottish Parliament.

Reference is made to a series of Work Streams which are scoped to run in some cases up to 2030. Some of the more straightforward proposals have been referred to at various parts of this work, and it is fair to describe these as fairly marginal if welcome in nature, and in the scheme of things, in the nature of low-hanging fruit.

Despite this, a number of likely influences can be discerned. The impact of the Human Rights Act 1998 has been extensive in the law of both the United Kingdom and Scotland, if not always comprehensive. One clear example of its influence is seen in the terms of the 2000 Act itself, where a considerable range of safeguards of vulnerable adults were created around a system of judicial authorisation, and a statutory regulator.

Nevertheless, as has been mentioned, matters such as the authorisation of the deprivation or restriction of liberty of such adults, or the separate regimes established under the 2000 and 2003 Acts – notwithstanding the cross over existing via the definition of “mental disorder” given there –

and the rate of detention of such adults raise very serious issues of whether the current law adequately respects the human rights of this sector of the population [3]. It may also be questioned whether the arrangements for the management of funds [4] is unduly onerous to the point where the regimes previously considered effectively are deterrents to their application.

It is important to note that despite the real possibility that the law in Scotland is – and has been for a considerable time – incompatible with the EConHR, in particular the deprivation of liberty of an incapable adult, the pace of change in key areas has been glacial in some instances. The decision of the Strasbourg Court in *Bournewood* was issued in 2003 [5]. The Scottish law commission presented its discussion paper *Adults with incapacity* [6] in 2012, which it followed with its *Report on adults with incapacity* [7] in 2014.

The Scott Report itself built upon a number of Reviews which had taken place prior to its publication in 2022. Despite this considerable thought and industry, the period during which aspects of the law in Scotland will have been in an unsatisfactory state at best is significant.

The wider context

It is possible to discern a range of possible significant influences on the form of law which may be proposed in the future. Respectively, these are:-

(a) <u>United Nations convention on the rights of persons with disability (CRPD)</u>

The CRPD was adopted by the United Nations in 2006 and signed by the United Kingdom in March 2007. It was formally ratified by the United Kingdom government on 8 June 2009.

In March 2021 the Scottish government announced its intention to implement the CRPD into Scottish law as part of a wider human rights bill. This decision resulted from consideration of a possible implementation process by the First minister's advisory group on human rights leadership which had issued the report *National task force for leadership* in the same month.

The form of the legislation effecting this process has not been specified. However, the recently – enacted United Nations Convention on the Rights of the Child (Incorporation) (Scotland) Bill has similarities to the 1998 Act, in terms of prohibiting public authorities from acting in a way incompatible with the provisions of the UNCRC cl.6, and the availability of judicial remedies (cls.7 & 8) for such breaches. Such drafting would be consistent with the recommendations of the *Taskforce on human rights leadership* also of March 2021.

If enacted, the legislation will adopt the overall principle underlying the CRPD can be summarised as follows: -

> A person with a "disability" is someone who has a:-
>
> "long – term physical mental, intellectual and sensory impairment of a long – term nature" [8]

Further, the CRPD states that:-

> "...All persons are equal before and under the law...[and the State] shall prohibit all discrimination on the basis of disability and guarantee to persons with disabilities equal and effective legal protection on all grounds" [9].

In the scope of the present work, it is not possible to explore fully the possible effects of such legislation on the current law, but amongst critical elements of the CRPD which the proposed human rights bill may give effect are:-

- Art.19 (Living independently and being included in the community)

- Art.23 (Respect for home and family)
- Art.24 (Right to education without discrimination)
- Art.25 (Right to the highest attainable standard of health without discrimination)

What may prove more difficult to express and apply legislatively are provisions to the effect that:-

> "1. States Parties reaffirm that persons with disabilities have the right to recognition everywhere as persons before the law.
>
> 2. States Parties shall recognize that persons with disabilities enjoy legal capacity on an equal basis with others in all aspects of life.
>
> 3. States Parties shall take appropriate measures to provide access by persons with disabilities to the support they may require in exercising their legal capacity.
>
> 4. States Parties shall ensure that all measures that relate to the exercise of legal capacity provide for appropriate and effective safeguards to prevent abuse in accordance with international human rights law. Such safeguards shall ensure that measures relating to the exercise of legal capacity respect the rights, will and preferences of the person, are free of conflict of interest and undue influence, are proportional and tailored to the person's circumstances, apply for the shortest time possible and are subject to regular review by a competent, independent and impartial authority or judicial body. The safeguards shall be proportional to the degree to which such measures affect the person's rights and interests" [10].

It is arguable, on the one hand, that the safeguards specified under art.12.4 are already reflected in the 2000 Act insofar as these "relate to the exercise of legal capacity". Against that, the terms of art.12.2 & 3, are claimed in some quarters to prohibit the continuation of substituted decision – making, as are articulated through measures such as guardianship [11].

It is important to bear in mind that an individual's "legal capacity" runs far wider than exercise of decision – making, and potentially extends into the formation use and termination of many kinds of legal relationships. Thus, one proposal is that a regime of supported decision – making and the interpretation of previous legal instruments, could be applied in an operable manner even when the adult lacks "capacity" [12].

As matters presently stand, the obligations of the Scottish government in this field will be informed by at least two human rights treaties with which it is obliged to comply. It is outside the scope of this work to make a comparison of the respective terms of the treaties. However, one important matter requiring to be resolved is an evident mismatch between the terms of art.14 of the CRPD that:-

> "States Parties shall ensure that persons with disabilities, on an equal basis with others:-
>
> a) enjoy the right to liberty and security of person;
>
> b) are not deprived of their liberty unlawfully or arbitrarily, and that any deprivation of liberty is in conformity with the law, and that the existence of a disability shall in no case justify a deprivation of liberty."

and Art.5.1 of the EConHR to the effect that:-

> "Everyone has the right to liberty and security of person. No one shall be deprived of his liberty save in the following cases and in accordance with a procedure prescribed by law…
>
> (a) the lawful detention of…. persons of unsound mind"

How a basis for authorising the deprivation of liberty of an incapable adult is determined by future legislation will be an important and instructive guide to the overall direction of the law in the future. At present, the law in Scotland appears to fall short of meeting either obligation [13].

At the time of writing, the thinking of the Scottish Government leans strongly in the direction of enshrining in law the primacy of the will and preferences of an incapable adult in all of the areas considered in this work, and particularly the operation of Powers of Attorney and Guardianships.

To a certain extent, reference to the CRPD can only have limited value. While the Scottish Government has indicated its intention to incorporate the CRPD into domestic law via a Scottish Human Rights Bill, the most recent indications are that this is not a matter of current priority. It cannot be said certainly that by 2030, the CRPD will be a directly enforceable instrument in Scotland.

(b) Mental Capacity (NI) Act 2016

The 2016 Act is notable for achieving a fusion of Mental Health and Mental Incapacity Law, for which there appears to be only muted enthusiasm in Scotland. That said, the Scottish Government is considering whether to adopt the formulation of the 2016 Act that an adult is not to be treated as unable to make a decision for themself unless all practicable help and support to enable the person to make decisions about the matter have been given without success [14].

Accordingly, consideration is also being given to whether "mental disorder" as currently defined [15] requires consideration in the light of modern thinking, and the CRPD particularly. Consultation is also in progress regarding a different treatment of certain neurodiversities via a Learning Disabilities, Neurodivergence and Autism Bill, which may see their removal from a future definition of "mental disorder"

### (c) Aspects of the Scottish Government's proposals

An important plank of the approach adopted by the Scottish Government is an increased emphasis on the will and preferences of an incapable adult. While this would apply particularly across matters such as the exercise of a Power of Attorney or Guardianship, it is proposed that the s.1(4) principles should be amended to give primacy to an adult's will and preferences. This is seen as an initial step towards the intended role of Decision-making Representative within a scheme of Human Rights Enablement, albeit how this is expressed in legislation remains unclear at time of writing.

Deprivation of Liberty

### (i) Non-Intervention

In extensive discussion of how a regime of Deprivation of Liberty could be introduced, the Scottish Government proposes to identify situations where an adult has sufficient Agency, or can with support, express their will and preferences, so as to agree to remain in their living situation – even where it would amount to a Deprivation of Liberty as a matter of law. Such circumstances would require no further judicial oversight in the first instance.

### (ii) Powers of Attorney

In situations where an Adult lacks – or at some point loses –capacity to agree to living in circumstances amounting to Deprivation of Liberty. The SG propose that a Power of Attorney should be permitted to grant advance consent to allow an Attorney to deprive the Adult of their liberty. Consequently, a considerable emphasis will fall on seeking to reliably show the loss of such capacity.

It is proposed, therefore, that loss of capacity will be established via independent medical assessment. In addition, Regulations will be introduced to provide safeguards set out in the text of an operable Power of Attorney to specify that:-

The granter has considered the circumstances in which it might be necessary to restrict their liberty or to deprive them of their liberty, in order to safeguard the granter's health or welfare or that of others

The terms of Art.5 of the Econ HR have been explained to the Granter

Authority passes to the Attorney(s) alone

The attorney must be satisfied the action is necessary to safeguard the health and welfare of the granter

The attorney must act in accordance with the principles of the 2000 Act

The Attorney will be subject to any directions of the court following any application under s.3(3) (c) of the 2000 Act.

The express reference to s.3(3) is designed to provide a clear means of challenge where an adult objects to some or all aspects of a deprivation of Liberty. A concomitant right would be that of challenging a deprivation of liberty by appeal to the Sheriff Court. As currently envisaged, the principal ground of challenge would be that the placement is not necessary to safeguard the health and wellbeing of the Adult. Any person other than the adult making such a challenge would require to demonstrate what steps have been taken to ascertain the views of the adult. It may be necessary for the Sheriff to consider appointment of a Safeguarder for that purpose.

A corollary to the authorisation of DOLS by an Attorney is the need for regular Review of the authority as required by Art.5.4 EConHR. At the time of writing, such a mechanism remains as a matter for future consultation.

(iii) Guardianship

In the case of Guardianship, the Scottish Government also propose that the Sheriff should be able to authorise a Guardian to place an Adult into a setting which amounts to a Deprivation of Liberty. This would be accompanied by provision for time limits of the authorisation and regular Review, and subject to an overall test that the measure should be a proportionate to the situation experienced by the Adult, whose will and preferences would be ascertained as part of the process

Both of the processes for authorising a Deprivation of Liberty of an adult would be subject to a right of Appeal to the Sheriff in the first instance. It is also proposed both that a standalone right of Appeal by any person "demonstrating an interest in the Adult", and also that the MWCS should have a specific power to investigate a DOL where referred by a person having an interest in the Adult or as the result of their own investigations

Medical Treatment

Some recognition of the potential vulnerability of an incapable adult where Medical Treatment is being provided is contained in the Scottish Government's proposals.

Any certificate issued under s.47 of the 2000 Act [16] would be initially time limited to 28 days and would also authorise measures to prevent the Adult leaving the hospital unaccompanied while the medical treatment is provided. Nevertheless, the clinician treating the Adult would be required to set a timescale for the measure and to consult with the Adult's Attorney or Guardian – where one is in place – when reviewing the necessity for the measures to remain in place. The Adult would have a right of Appeal against the order with access to practical and active assistance in so doing.

A criterion of alleviating "serious suffering" on the part of an Adult is proposed to be added to the circumstances where power under s.50 is exercised by a medical practitioner in the absence of an interdict [17]. Extensive proposals for reform of authorisation of the involvement of incapable adults in Medical Research and Clinical Drugs Trials are also set out.

## Conclusion

It is important to appreciate that more aspects of the law outlined in this text is subject to expert and extensive consideration at the time of writing. The final outcome of this process is still some way in the distance, and ultimately may find itself choosing between radical and fundamental change or for modifying the current system in order to reflect the outcome of an extensive consultation process.

This does not necessarily imply that the law in Scotland is moving away from Substitute decision making, as some argue the CRPD mandates, but one proposal which will be subject to consultation is a change to the s.1 (4) principles to give primacy in their application to an adult's will and preferences.

There is, of course, proper space to be accorded to the public and to incapable adults and their families, as well as to experts and politicians to have their say on the acceptability of what the Scottish Government has and will propose. Nevertheless, the announced direction of travel is towards incorporation of human rights treaties into our law, and unquestionably this will drive changes which bring the law closer to achieving equality and non – discrimination in its application to adults with disability.

Seen in this perspective, a somewhat different version of this work seems likely to be required by later in the present decade. It is realistic at least to see a 2030 Act as being framed in very different – and possibly radically different – terms to the 2000 Act. What such an imagined piece of legislation will actually contain is, for now, a matter for conjecture.

## NOTES (CHAPTER 24)

1. mentalhealthlawreview.scot.

2. https://www.gov.scot/publications/scottish-mental-health-law-review-response/

3. See Chapter 20 above.

4. See Chapter 16 above.

5. See Chapter 20 above.

6. *Adults with Incapacity*, SLC discussion paper No.156 (2012).

7. *Report on Adults with Incapacity*, SLC report No.240 (2014, Chapter 6. See Chapter 20 above.

8. CRPD, Art 1.

9. CRPD, Arts 5.1 & 5.2.

10. CRPD, Art.12.

11. See UN committee on the CRPD, general comment No.1 (2014), paras.3 & 28, and the consideration of 2000 Act, s.67 (1) at Chapter 10 above.

12. Essex autonomy project report (2016), para.6.1. See also the consideration of "collaborative decision making" as applied in the Australian state of Victoria in the SLC Discussion Paper 156, *Adults with Incapacity*.

13. See Chapter 20 above.

14. Mental Capacity (NI) Act 2016. ss.3-4).

15. Mental Health (Care and Treatment) (Scotland) Act 2003, s.328.

16. See Chapter 23 above.

17. See Mental Health (Care and Treatment) (Scotland) Act 2003. s.243 (3) (c).

# MORE BOOKS BY LAW BRIEF PUBLISHING

A selection of our other titles available now:-

| |
|---|
| 'A Practical Guide to Probation Breaches and Other Applications' by Mark Thomas |
| 'A Practical Guide to Remarriage and Divorce' by Cordelia Williams & Claire Howard |
| 'A Practical Guide to Privacy, Transparency, Reporting Restrictions and Closed Proceedings in the Court of Protection' by Laura Mannering |
| 'Beaumont on Barristers – A Guide to Defending Disciplinary Proceedings (Second Edition)' by Marc Beaumont |
| 'A Practical Guide to Payments for Environmental Services' by Ben Sharples |
| 'A Practical Guide to the Law of Pregnancy and Maternity at Work' by Rebecca Thomas |
| 'A Practical Guide to Redundancy – Second Edition' by Philip Hyland & Collette Moore |
| 'A Practical Guide to International Issues for Scottish Family Lawyers' by Susie Mountain, Donna McKay, Ken MacDonald |
| 'A Practical Guide to the Law on Deprivation of Liberty' by Ben Troke |
| 'A Practical Guide to Rights over Airspace and Subsoil – Second Edition' by Daniel Gatty |
| 'A Practical Guide to the Law in Relation to Inquests' by Ramya Nagesh |
| 'A Practical Guide to the Construction and Rectification of Wills and Trust Instruments (Second Edition)' by Edward Hewitt |
| 'A Practical Guide to Data Protection in Social Housing' by Clare Paterson |
| 'A Practical Guide to Spousal Maintenance – Second Edition' by Liz Cowell |
| 'A Practical Guide to International Parental Child Abduction Law (England and Wales)' by Dr Onyója Momoh |
| 'A Practical Guide to Deprivation of British Citizenship' by Sean Ell |
| 'A Practical Guide to Commercial Property Service Charges' by Rachel Garton |
| 'A Practical Guide to Clinical Negligence – Third Edition' by Geoffrey Simpson-Scott (Geoff) |
| 'A Practical Guide to the Rights of Grandparents in Children Proceedings – Second Edition' by Stuart Barlow |

| |
|---|
| 'The Electronic Communications Code: A Practical Guide – Second Edition' by Kerry Bretherton KC, James Castle, Mark Loveday |
| 'A Practical Guide to the Independent School Standards – September 2023 Edition' by Sarah McKimm |
| 'A Practical Guide to Estate Administration and Crypto Assets' by Richard Marshall |
| 'A Practical Guide to Parental Alienation in Private and Public Law Children Cases' by Sam King QC & Frankie Shama |
| 'Contested Heritage – Removing Art from Land and Historic Buildings' by Richard Harwood QC, Catherine Dobson, David Sawtell |
| 'The Limits of Separate Legal Personality: When Those Running a Company Can Be Held Personally Liable for Losses Caused to Third Parties Outside of the Company' by Dr Mike Wilkinson |
| 'A Practical Guide to Transgender Law' by Robin Moira White & Nicola Newbegin |
| 'A Practical Guide to 'Stranded Spouses' in Family Law' by Mani Singh Basi |
| 'A Practical Guide to Residential Freehold Conveyancing' by Lorraine Richardson |
| 'A Practical Guide to Pensions on Divorce for Lawyers' by Bryan Scant |
| 'A Practical Guide to Challenging Sham Marriage Allegations in Immigration Law' by Priya Solanki |
| 'A Practical Guide to Digital Communications Evidence in Criminal Law' by Sam Willis |
| 'A Practical Guide to Legal Rights in Scotland' by Sarah-Jane Macdonald |
| 'A Practical Guide to New Build Conveyancing' by Paul Sams & Rebecca East |
| 'A Practical Guide to Inherited Wealth on Divorce' by Hayley Trim |
| 'A Practical Guide to Practice Direction 12J and Domestic Abuse in Private Law Children Proceedings' by Rebecca Cross & Malvika Jaganmohan |
| 'A Practical Guide to Confiscation and Restraint' by Narita Bahra QC, John Carl Townsend, David Winch |
| 'A Practical Guide to the Law of Forests in Scotland' by Philip Buchan |
| 'A Practical Guide to Health and Medical Cases in Immigration Law' by Rebecca Chapman & Miranda Butler |
| 'A Practical Guide to Bad Character Evidence for Criminal Practitioners by Aparna Rao |
| 'A Practical Guide to Extradition Law post-Brexit' by Myles Grandison et al |
| 'A Practical Guide to Hoarding and Mental Health for Housing Lawyers' by Rachel Coyle |

| |
|---|
| 'Stephens on Contractual Indemnities' by Richard Stephens |
| 'A Practical Guide to the EU Succession Regulation' by Richard Frimston |
| 'A Practical Guide to Solicitor and Client Costs – Second Edition' by Robin Dunne |
| 'Constructive Dismissal – Practice Pointers and Principles' by Benjimin Burgher |
| 'A Practical Guide to Religion and Belief Discrimination Claims in the Workplace' by Kashif Ali |
| 'A Practical Guide to the Law of Medical Treatment Decisions' by Ben Troke |
| 'Fundamental Dishonesty and QOCS in Personal Injury Proceedings: Law and Practice' by Jake Rowley |
| 'A Practical Guide to the Law in Relation to School Exclusions' by Charlotte Hadfield & Alice de Coverley |
| 'A Practical Guide to Divorce for the Silver Separators' by Karin Walker |
| 'The Right to be Forgotten – The Law and Practical Issues' by Melissa Stock |
| 'A Practical Guide to Planning Law and Rights of Way in National Parks, the Broads and AONBs' by James Maurici QC, James Neill et al |
| 'A Practical Guide to Election Law' by Tom Tabori |
| 'A Practical Guide to the Law in Relation to Surrogacy' by Andrew Powell |
| 'A Practical Guide to Claims Arising from Fatal Accidents – Second Edition' by James Patience |
| 'A Practical Guide to Asbestos Claims' by Jonathan Owen & Gareth McAloon |
| 'A Practical Guide to Stamp Duty Land Tax in England and Northern Ireland' by Suzanne O'Hara |
| 'A Practical Guide to the Law of Farming Partnerships' by Philip Whitcomb |
| 'A Practical Guide to the Law of Unlawful Eviction and Harassment – Second Edition' by Stephanie Lovegrove |
| 'A Practical Guide to Costs in Personal Injury Claims – Second Edition' by Matthew Hoe |
| 'A Practical Guide to the General Data Protection Regulation (GDPR) – Second Edition' by Keith Markham |
| 'A Practical Guide to Working with Litigants in Person and McKenzie Friends in Family Cases' by Stuart Barlow |
| 'Protecting Unregistered Brands: A Practical Guide to the Law of Passing Off' by Lorna Brazell |
| 'A Practical Guide to Secondary Liability and Joint Enterprise Post-Jogee' by Joanne Cecil & James Mehigan |

| |
|---|
| 'A Practical Guide to the Pre-Action RTA Claims Protocol for Personal Injury Lawyers' by Antonia Ford |
| 'A Practical Guide to Neighbour Disputes and the Law' by Alexander Walsh |
| 'A Practical Guide to Coercive Control for Legal Practitioners and Victims' by Rachel Horman |
| 'A Practical Guide to the Law of Driverless Cars – Second Edition' |
| by Alex Glassbrook, Emma Northey & Scarlett Milligan |
| 'A Practical Guide to TOLATA Claims' by Greg Williams |
| 'A Practical Guide to Elderly Law – Second Edition' by Justin Patten |
| 'A Practical Guide to Responding to Housing Disrepair and Unfitness Claims' by Iain Wightwick |
| 'A Practical Guide to the Law of Bullying and Harassment in the Workplace' by Philip Hyland |
| 'How to Be a Freelance Solicitor: A Practical Guide to the SRA-Regulated Freelance Solicitor Model' by Paul Bennett |
| 'A Practical Guide to Prison Injury Claims' by Malcolm Johnson |
| 'A Practical Guide to Advising Clients at the Police Station' by Colin Stephen McKeown-Beaumont |
| 'A Practical Guide to Antisocial Behaviour Injunctions – Second Edition' by Iain Wightwick |
| 'Practical Mediation: A Guide for Mediators, Advocates, Advisers, Lawyers, and Students in Civil, Commercial, Business, Property, Workplace, and Employment Cases' by Jonathan Dingle with John Sephton |
| 'The Mini-Pupillage Workbook' by David Boyle |
| 'A Practical Guide to Crofting Law' by Brian Inkster |
| 'A Practical Guide to the Law of Domain Names and Cybersquatting' by Andrew Clemson |
| 'A Practical Guide to the Law of Gender Pay Gap Reporting' by Harini Iyengar |
| 'NHS Whistleblowing and the Law' by Joseph England |
| 'Employment Law and the Gig Economy' by Nigel Mackay & Annie Powell |
| 'A Practical Guide to Noise Induced Hearing Loss (NIHL) Claims' by Andrew Mckie, Ian Skeate, Gareth McAloon |
| 'An Introduction to Beauty Negligence Claims – A Practical Guide for the Personal Injury Practitioner' by Greg Almond |
| 'Intercompany Agreements for Transfer Pricing Compliance' by Paul Sutton |
| 'Zen and the Art of Mediation' by Martin Plowman |
| 'A Practical Guide to Adoption for Family Lawyers' by Graham Pegg |

www.ingramcontent.com/pod-product-compliance
Lightning Source LLC
LaVergne TN
LVHW052307200926
848481LV00002B/486
* 9 7 8 1 9 1 6 6 9 8 6 3 5 *